A Scripture Index to John Milton's *De doctrina christiana*

medieval & renaissance
texts & studies

Volume 67

A Scripture Index to John Milton's *De doctrina christiana*

by

MICHAEL BAUMAN

medieval & renaissance texts & studies
Binghamton, New York
1989

Library of Congress Cataloging-in-Publication Data

Bauman, Michael,
A scripture index to John Milton's De doctrina christiana / by Michael Bauman.
p. cm. — (Medieval & Renaissance texts & studies ; v. 67)
Includes index.
ISBN 0-86698-076-8
1. Milton, John, 1608-1674—Religion. 2. Milton, John, 1608-1674. De doctrina christiana—Indexes. 3. Bible in literature—Indexes. I. Title. II. Series.
PR3592.R4B37 1989
230—dc19 89-3107
CIP

This book is made to last.
It is set in Trump Medieval, smythe-sewn,
and printed on acid-free paper
to library specifications.

Printed in the United States of America

For

Maurice Kelley,

who has spent more time with

the De doctrina christiana *than did*

either Daniel Skinner or Jeremie Picard

[I] have striven to cram my pages even to overflowing, with quotations drawn from all parts of the Bible and to leave as little space as possible for my own words. . . .

[T]he only authority I accepted was God's self-revelation, and accordingly I read and pondered the Holy Scriptures themselves with all possible diligence, never sparing myself in any way.

John Milton, *De doctrina christiana*

Contents

Introduction 9

The Index

Old Testament 15

Apocrypha 88

New Testament 89

Notes 161

Tables 173

A Scripture Index to John Milton's *De doctrina christiana*

Introduction

This book aims to provide a comprehensive, accurate, and convenient index to the many scriptural passages which are quoted, cited, or alluded to in Milton's *De doctrina christiana*. In so doing, it will fill a notable gap in available research tools.

Milton opted to "cram [his] pages, even to overflowing, with quotations drawn from all parts of the Bible,"[1] unlike those who filled their pages almost entirely with expositions of their own ideas, and banished the Bible to their margins. Milton was a man of his word and a man of the Word. He had said that he would write his theological treatise in a new way, and even the most casual observer can see that he did so. After nearly twenty years of studying Christian doctrine, I have discovered no systematic theology, Protestant or other, that is even remotely as biblically grounded as Milton's. For page after page, the range and number of his biblical references easily outstrip those of every other comparable text.

Though Milton claims to derive his theology "from the word of God and from that alone,"[2] in those very chapters where his views are most unorthodox, his frequency of biblical citation is lowest. As a rule, in such chapters, his biblical quotations are more sparsely scattered and his argument is advanced more fully in his own words and by means of his philosophical constructs than is the case in the more orthodox chapters. For example, his antitrinitarian chapter on the Son of God (bk. I, chap. 5), which is his longest chapter (78 pages in the Yale edition), is also one of the chapters with the lowest citational frequency—10.2 citations per page. He resorts to scripture even less frequently when he explicates his eccentric views on marriage (bk. I, chap. 10: 2.1 citations per page) and on the sabbath (bk. II, chap. 7: 7.2 citations per page). By contrast, the frequency of his biblical citations is significantly greater in chapters where the views he is expressing are more widely accepted, as they are on such topics as reciprocal and private moral duties (bk. II, chap. 15: 30.6 citations per page), public moral duties (bk. II, chap. 17: 25.6 citations per page), and duties toward one's neighbor (bk. II, chap. 12: 25.2 citations per page).

This wealth of citation supports Milton's statement that the *De doctrina christiana* derives from an antecedent theological commonplace book.[3] Even if we did not know of such a book, after scrutinizing Milton's use of the Bible in this treatise we could reasonably have supposed its existence. Milton's treatise appears clearly to be the descendant of a theological index. The same biblical verses often occur together as if they were gathered under the same heading and brought out in a group each time that topic was addressed. Milton apparently has arranged several constellations or clusters of biblical passages which he uses as an entity. To cite but four typical examples, every reference to Genesis 22:18 is accompanied by a reference to Genesis 3:15. Colossians 3:9–11 forms a consistent citational constellation with Ephesians 4:22–24. Acts 20:28 and Matthew 20:28 tend to occur in tandem, as do Psalm 51:10 and Ezekiel 11:19.

All these considerations point to the need for a comprehensive, accurate, and convenient index.

The Yale edition of *De doctrina* has no index. The Columbia edition has an index, but it is incomplete, sometimes inaccurate, and hard to use, because it is organized by the order in which the quotations occur in Milton's treatise rather than by their biblical sequence.[4] Thus, to determine whether Milton treated a particular verse or passage of Galatians, and to examine his exegesis of this text, one would need first to read through all Galatians references in the Columbia index. Furthermore, the Columbia index is keyed not to Milton's Latin text but to Sumner's notorious 1825 translation, which silently employs a verse numbering system different from that which Milton used in his Latin original, and which often adopts the AV translation rather than translating Milton's actual Latin text.

As a tool for research, then, this index is long overdue. Six decades ago, Harris Fletcher tried to supply Miltonists with such an index in *The Use of the Bible in Milton's Prose.*[5] But while Fletcher's index follows biblical order, it has two drawbacks. It is keyed to Sumner's 1825 Latin edition, which is neither definitive nor readily accessible; and it was completed before the publication of either the Columbia or Yale editions of Milton's work, and therefore can not be used with either of these editions. Too often, furthermore, it is incomplete, inaccurate, or misleading.

The present index corrects Fletcher. It also corrects a number of erroneous citations in the Columbia and Yale editions, and it includes many previously unidentified allusions to scripture.

Organization

While compiling this index, I have tried always to keep before me the varied considerations of accuracy, simplicity, utility, and completeness.

1. The index is arranged in biblical sequence, with references to a chapter in general placed before references to individual verses within that chapter. That is, a reference to Genesis 1 precedes a reference to Genesis 1:1. In most places where Milton refers to a passage consisting of more than one verse, each verse in that passage is listed separately, unless otherwise noted. Thus, if Milton has quoted 2 Corinthians 2:6–8, each of the three verses in the passage is listed.

   The numbering of biblical verses presents particular problems in itself. The Authorized Version occasionally diverges from the Junius-Tremellius text, and Milton—who was presumably working from the latter[6]—also numbers differently from the AV. For example, many of the Psalms are prefaced by a superscription which is numbered in Junius-Tremellius but not in the AV. Thus, a scholar looking for Milton's treatment of Psalm 51.3 in the AV would need to look for Psalm 51.5 in the *De doctrina christiana*. To untangle this ambiguity, I have listed all passages according to their modern Authorized Version designation and cited any variations in brackets.

2. The index is arranged in three columns. The first column identifies the specific biblical passage or verse. (If Fletcher's index omits the reference, I have so indicated by the symbol °.) The other two columns are given to the Columbia University Press Latin edition of Milton's text and to the Yale University Press English translation. When either Columbia or Yale is mistaken, I have indicated this in the notes.

   For references to the Columbia Latin edition, I have included both a volume and a page number, referring to the four volumes which comprise that edition of Milton's systematic theology.

That is, 14:126 means that the citation can be found in volume 14, on page 126. Corresponding English citations in Columbia are not noted in this index because they are easily found on the facing pages in Sumner's English translation.

For the Yale edition, no volume is cited because all references are to be found in volume 6. The Yale edition itself indicates the original manuscript page for each entry.

3. Citational inconsistencies (inevitable with 9000 references) are noted, and in places where it seemed useful, I have offered a brief explanation in the notes. For example, when Milton cites the location but not the verse itself, I have noted this fact. When he quotes a verse but does not cite its location, I have identified it, placed it in its proper location in the index, and used the symbol ᑫ to call attention to this.[7] Or if Milton cites two verses but quotes from only one, I have noted this if it seems to merit notice. I have tried to err on the side of safety in noting anything about which there might be doubt or special significance.

4. Allusions are far more difficult to treat accurately than are citations. I have preferred to omit faint allusions rather than to include false ones, or ones which might be ringing only in my ears. Bearing in mind, therefore, the sometimes subjective nature of this process, I have taken a conservative approach.

5. In addition to indexing Milton's scriptural citations, I have included three tables. The first computes the number of Milton's biblical citations and arranges them according to their distribution, chapter by chapter, in his text. The second table lists those biblical verses most often cited by Milton, including any verse cited five or more times. The final table compares the number of Milton's biblical citations with John Calvin's in his *Institutes of the Christian Religion*, and arranges them by canonical book.

Though I have taken great care to make this index as accurate as possible, I cannot but believe that in the complicated process of reading, evaluating, transcribing, typing and proofreading this text, lapses will have occurred. Along with a previous student of Milton's systematic theology, I can only say that the "perfect execution of this undertaking would require the eyes of Lynceus and the ants of Psyche—neither of which is at my command."[8]

Acknowledgements

I wish to acknowledge the kindness of those who assisted me in the tedious work of compiling this index. Ferris McDaniel, of Columbia Bible College and Seminary, unselfishly laid his knowledge of the Bible at my disposal and often helped to identify obscure references to what, for me at least, were forgotten corners in the Old Testament and Apocrypha. I am indebted also to John Peter Rumrich, of the University of Texas at Austin, for introducing me to Milton studies in general, and for suggesting this project in particular. This is now the second book on Milton that his guidance and encouragement have helped me bring to completion. Nor can I adequately acknowledge the scope of my wife's contribution to this project. She had the truly unenviable task not only of typing the entire manuscript twice, but of helping me to proofread it. If this index, therefore, proves to be of use, thank her.

Finally, my greatest and most enduring debt as a student of Milton I proudly and gratefully acknowledge in the dedication.

Michael Bauman

Hillsdale College
Hillsdale, Michigan
April 1989

Notes

1. John Milton, *The Complete Prose Works of John Milton*, gen. ed., Don M. Wolfe (New Haven: Yale University Press, 1953–82), 6:122. Hereafter cited as Yale.
2. Yale, 120.
3. See Yale, 119, and Maurice Kelley's useful explanation, Yale, 16 ff.
4. John Milton, *The Works of John Milton*, gen. ed., Frank Allen Patterson, 18 vols. (New York: Columbia University Press, 1931–38), vols. 14–17.
5. Harris F. Fletcher, *The Use of the Bible in Milton's Prose* (New York: Haskell House, 1975, reprint of 1929 edition).
6. See Yale, 579 n. 11; 582 n. 18; and Fletcher, 82 ff.
7. In nearly every instance where Milton quotes a verse without citing its location, or else merely alludes to a verse, the Columbia index omits the reference.
8. Yale, 809.

The Index

Old Testament Apocrypha

Symbols

[o] Fletcher *omits* this reference.

[c] Milton *cites* this verse but does not quote it.

[q] Milton *quotes* this verse but does not cite it.

[x] Milton quotes this verse but does not give its *exact* location.

Old Testament

TEXT	COLUMBIA EDITION	YALE EDITION

Genesis

TEXT	COLUMBIA EDITION	YALE EDITION
1	15:6, 36, 66	301, 315, 330
1:1[1]	14:52	148
1:2	14:358; 15:12–14	282, 304–305
1:21	15:16	306
1:22	15:42–44	320 [1:21]
1:26	14:34; 15:36	135, 316
1:27	15:16, 52	306, 324
1:28	15:42–44, 112	320, 351
1:30	15:42	319
1:31	15:14, 52	305, 324
2:1	15:32	313
2:2	15:42, 116; 17:168[c]	319, 353, 705[c]
2:3	15:42, 116; 17:168[c]	319, 353, 705[c]
2:7	15:38, 38–40[q]	317, 317[q]
2:15	15:112; 17:230	351, 731
2:16	15:112	351
2:17	14:110; 15:112, 178–180, 202, 226[2]	178, 351, 382, 393, 404[3]
2:18	15:120, 156[4]	355, 371
2:20	15:52, 156[5]	324, 371
2:22	15:44; 17:352	320, 782
2:24	15:120–122, 122–124, 134, 154	355, 356, 361, 370
2:25	15:52	324
3:[o]	15:180	383
3:4	17:300[c]	760[c]
3:6	15:180	382
3:7	15:202, 204 (twice)	393–394, 394 (twice)
3:8	15:204	394
3:14	15:216	399
3:15	15:252, 256, 258, 344; 16:98, 116[c]	416, 418 (twice), 454, 515, 523[c]

3:16	15:120[6], 182, 214; 16:326[c]; 17:352	355[7], 384, 399, 609[c], 782
3:17	15:214, 216	399 (twice)
3:19	15:214; 17:230	399, 731
3:22	15:114	353
3:24	15:36, 102	315, 346
4	17:266 (twice)	746, 747
4:3	16:102	516
4:4	16:30, 102[c]	487, 516[c]
4:7	14:110; 17:364	178, 786
4:9	17:300[c]	760[c]
4:10	17:284	754
4:13	15:358; 17:58	458, 659
4:26	16:102	516
5:3	14:34; 15:44	135–136, 320
5:24	16:30, 336[c]	487, 614[c]
6	15:154	370
6:2	16:50; 17:202–204	494, 720
6:3	14:358	282
6:4	14:44	143
6:5	14:54; 15:194	149, 389
6:6	14:32, 34	134, 135
6:7	15:216	399
6:8	16:30, 46	487, 493
6:9	16:22, 46	483, 493
7:1	16:30[c], 102	487[c], 516
7:2	16:102	516
7:22	15:42	319
8:1	15:62	329
8:20	16:102	516
8:21	14:62[c]; 15:194; 16:102[c]	154[c], 389, 516[c]
9	17:214	725
9:2	15:208	396
9:5	17:284[c]	754[c]
9:6	15:208; 17:284, 388	396, 754, 795
9:9	15:62	329
9:10	15:62	329
9:12	15:62	329
9:15	15:62	329
9:16	14:284	252
9:22	17:356	784
9:23	17:356	783
9:25	15:190; 17:98	387, 675
12:1	15:350	455
12:3	17:102–104, 274	677, 750
12:4	16:102[c]; 17:68 [12:1]	516[c], 663 [12:1]

12:5	16:102[c]	516[c]
12:13	17:54[8], 240[c], 300[c]	658[9], 735[c], 760[c]
12:15	17:392	796
12:17[o]	15:188 [12:14]	386 [12:14]
13:8	17:274, 364	749, 786
13:9	17:342	778
13:15	16:368[c]	627[c]
13:18	16:102[c]	516[c]
14:12	17:278	751
14:13	17:404[c]	801[c]
14:21	17:24[c]	646[c]
14:22	14:46–48; 17:120, 240[c]	145, 684, 735[c]
14:23	17:120, 240[c]	684, 735[c]
15:1	17:10	640
15:6	16:30, 38	487, 490
15:16	14:164[c]	199[c]
16:1	15:146	366
16:4	17:370	788
16:6	17:368	787
16:7	14:278	251
16:9	17:368	788
16:10	14:278	251
16:13	14:278	251
17	16:180	548
17:1	14:22, 46; 15:346; 16:22, 46; 17:38	128, 145, 454, 483, 493, 652
17:7	15:44; 16:174	320, 546
17:8	16:174[c]	546[c]
17:9	16:174[c]	546[c]
17:10	16:164, 198	542, 555
17:11	16:164[q], 198	542[q], 555
17:12	17:368	787
17:13	16:368[c]	627[c]
18:2	17:294	758
18:13[o]	14:278 [18:10]	251 [18:10]
18:14	14:54	149
18:15	17:300[c]	760[c]
18:19	17:348	781
18:26	17:274–276	750
19	17:214	725
19:1	14:278	251
19:5	17:290	756
19:12[o]	17:278	751
19:13	14:278; 15:102	251, 346
19:17	14:64	155
19:18[10]	14:278	251

19:21	14:64, 278; 17:276	155, 251, 750
19:24	14:278, 282	251, 252
19:26	17:32[c]	650[c]
20	17:300	760
20:3	17:292	757
20:7	15:188; 16:244; 17:276	386, 572, 750
20:12	17:292	757
20:13	14:246	236
20:14	17:240[c]	735[c]
21:8	17:234	732
21:10	15:170	377
21:12	15:170	377
21:14	15:170	377
21:17	14:248[c], 278	237[c], 251
21:18	14:248[c], 278	237[c], 251
21:27	17:404[c]	801[c]
21:33	14:42	143
22:3	17:68	663
22:5	17:304[c]	763[c]
22:11	14:248[c]	237[c]
22:12	14:248[c]	237[c]
22:15	14:248[c]	237[c]
22:16	14:248; 17:120	237, 684
22:18	15:256–258, 344; 16:116[c]	418, 454, 523[c]
23:[o,11]	16:38	490
23:7	17:294	758
23:8	17:262	744
23:13	17:240[c]	735[c]
23:19	17:262[c]	745[c]
24:3	17:130–132	689
24:9	17:368–370	788
24:15	17:356	783
24:22	17:234	733
25:22	16:102[c]	516[c]
25:28	17:354	783
26:4	15:258	418
26:29	17:404[c]	801[c]
26:30	17:404[c]	801[c]
26:31	15:128, 130[12]; 17:404[c]	359, 360[13], 801[c]
27	17:306	763
27:40[o]	14:160 [27:42]	198 [27:42]
27:41[o]	17:266[c] [27:43]	746[c] [27:43]
28:12	14:250; 15:100	237, 345
28:13	14:250	237
28:14	15:258	418

28:18	16:102[c]	516[c]
28:20	17:110	680
29:9	17:356	783
29:11	17:364	786
29:13	17:364	786
30	15:146	366
31:11	14:248	237
31:12	14:248	237
31:13	14:248	237
31:53	17:120	684
32:1	15:104	347
32:2	15:104	347
32:7	17:54, 208	658, 722
32:10	17:64	661
32:29	17:32	650
32:30	14:248, 250	237 (twice)
33:10	14:162	198
34:[o]	17:78	668
34:1	17:290[c]	756[c]
34:2[o]	17:290[x]	756[x]
35:2[o]	16:102	516
35:14	16:102[c]	516[c]
35:18	17:262[c]	745[c]
35:20	17:262	744
37:2	17:326	771
37:35	15:220	401
38:9	17:218[c]	727[c]
38:10	17:218	727
38:24	17:292	757
41	17:242	735
41:27	16:200	555
41:38	14:362	283
42:7	17:306[c]	763[c]
42:15	17:130	688
42:16	17:130	688
42:21	17:42	653
42:24	17:206	721
42:36	15:220	401
43:33	17:364	786
45:5	15:68	331
45:8	15:78–80	335
46:26	15:44	320
47:29	17:132	689
48:7	17:262[c]	745[c]
48:15	14:394; 17:146[c]	295, 695[c]

48:16	14:288, 394; 17:146	254, 295, 695
49:3	15:8	302
49:10	15:258, 282 (twice); 16:116[c]	418, 428, 429, 523[c]
49:29	17:262[c]	745[c]
50:2	17:262	744
50:3	17:260	744
50:10	17:260	744
50:20	15:68	331
50:25	17:262[c]	745[c]

Exodus

1:17	17:400	799
1:19	17:306[c]	763[c]
2:2	17:400	799
2:14	17:208	722
2:16	17:356	783
3	17:306, 402[1]	763, 800[2]
3:2	14:278	251
3:4	14:278	251
3:8	14:64	155
3:11	17:236	733
3:14	14:40 (twice)[3]	138, 140[4]
3:15	14:38, 40[c]	138–139, 140[c]
3:17	14:64	155
3:19	14:162	198
3:21	15:62	329
4:16	14:244[c]	234[c]
4:21	15:70	331
4:22	14:190	211
4:24	14:64–66[c]; 16:210	155[c], 559
4:25	16:210; 17:352	559, 782
4:26	16:180[c], 210	548[c], 559
5:2	15:80	336
6:3	14:40	139
6:6	15:94	341
6:7	15:94	341
6:8[o]	17:120 [6:7]	684 [6:7]
6:20	17:292	757
7:1	14:244[c]	235[c]
7:2	15:80	336
7:3	15:70 [7:6], 80–82	331 [7:6], 336
8:22	15:94	341
9:16	15:68, 82	331, 337

9:27	15:358	458
9:34	15:82–84	337
10:2	15:82	337
11	17:306	763
11:5	15:216	399
11:8	17:324	770
12	17:306	763
12:3	16:166	543
12:11	16:198	555
12:13	16:166–168	543
12:15	16:168	543
13:5	16:210	559
14:4	15:82	337
14:15	17:86	671
14:17	15:82; 17:408	337, 802
14:18	17:408[c]	802[c]
14:31	14:332	271
15:11	14:56	150
15:20	16:244[c]	572[c]
16:[o]	15:118; 17:168	354, 705
16:1[o]	17:168[c]	705[c]
16:5	15:118[c]	354[c]
16:22	15:118[c]	354[c]
16:23[o]	15:118[c]; 17:168 (twice)[5]	354[c], 705 (twice)[6]
16:24	15:118[c]	354[c]
16:25[o]	15:118[c]; 17:168[c]	354[c], 705[c]
16:26	15:118[c]	354[c]
16:27[o]	15:118[c]	354[c]
16:28[o]	15:118[c]	354[c]
16:29[o]	15:118[c]; 17:168[c]	354[c], 705[c]
16:30	15:118 (twice)[7]	354 (twice)[8]
16:33[o]	16:116 [16:34]	354 [16:34]
16:34	15:116 [16:35]	354 [16:35]
17:5	16:102[c]	516[c]
17:7	17:148	695
17:16	14:40; 17:288	138, 755
18:7	17:294, 356	758, 784
18:12	16:240[c]	571[c]
18:14	17:276	750
18:21	17:388	795
18:24	17:276	750
19:5	16:104	517
19:6	16:104, 244[c]	517, 572[c]
19:10	15:374	464
19:18	14:60	151

19:22	16:240	571
19:23	17:32	650
20	14:278	251
20:2[o]	17:184[q]	711[q]
20:3[o]	14:244	234
20:4	17:134	691
20:5	15:184; 17:134	385, 691
20:6	17:22[c]	645[c]
20:7	14:38; 17:120, 154	138, 685, 698
20:8	17:168	705
20:11	17:170[c]	705[c]
20:12	15:92; 17:356	340, 784
20:13	17:284	754
20:14	17:290	756
20:15	17:330	773
20:16	17:310	764
20:17	15:124, 198; 17:282	357, 391, 753
20:26	17:222	728
21:1	15:160	373
21:2	15:160; 17:368[c]	373, 788[c]
21:3	15:160; 17:368[c]	373, 788[c]
21:4	15:158, 160; 17:368[c]	372, 373, 788[c]
21:6	14:244	234
21:10	15:134, 136 (twice), 158, 160–162; 17:348–350	362 (twice), 363, 372, 373–374, 781
21:11	15:158, 160–162; 17:348–350	372, 373–374, 781
21:12	17:284	754
21:13	15:64, 66	329, 330
21:14	17:284–286	754
21:15	17:356	784
21:16	17:334	774
21:17	17:358	784
21:18	17:286	755
21:20	17:368	788
21:21	17:368[c]	788[c]
21:26	17:366, 368[c]	787, 788[c]
21:27	17:366[c], 368[c]	787[c], 788[c]
21:28	17:286	754
21:33	17:332–334	774
21:35	17:334	774
21:36	17:334	774
22	17:330	773
22:5	17:334	774
22:6	17:334[c]	774[c]
22:7	17:342	778

22:8	14:244[c]	234[c]
22:9	14:244[c]	234[c]
22:10	17:342[c]	778[c]
22:11	17:342[c]	778[c]
22:14	17:336	775
22:15	17:336	775
22:16	17:290	756
22:17	15:152; 17:290[c]	368, 756[c]
22:18	17:148	696
22:19	17:218	727
22:21	17:382[c]	793[c]
22:22	17:376	790
22:23	17:376[c]	790[c]
22:24	17:376[c]	790[c]
22:25	17:338, 340[9]	775, 777[10]
22:26	17:342	778
22:28	14:244[c]; 17:398	234[c], 799
23:1	17:310, 312	764–765, 766
23:4	17:256	742
23:5	17:256[c]	742[c]
23:8	17:384	794
23:10	17:372[c]	789[c]
23:11	17:372	789
23:12	17:172	706
23:17[11]	14:246	236
23:20	14:286, 290	253, 255
23:21	14:286, 290, 296	253, 255, 257
23:32	17:404	801
23:33	17:404[c]	801[c]
24:5	16:240	571
24:10	14:60, 248; 17:138	151, 237, 691–692
24:11	14:248; 17:138	237, 692
24:17	17:138	692
31:13	15:374; 17:172, 176[c]	464, 706, 708[c]
31:14	17:168, 172[x], 176[c]	705, 706[x], 708[c]
31:16	16:368[c]; 17:170 [31:15]	627[c], 705 [31:15]
31:17	14:34; 15:116; 17:170, 180	135, 353, 705–706, 709
32:5	17:136	691
32:10	17:100	676
32:11	17:384	794
32:19	17:152[c]	697[c]
32:27	17:258	743
32:32	14:110	178
32:33	14:110	178
33	15:30	312

33:2	14:288	254
33:3	14:288	254
33:5	14:288	254
33:9	14:60	151
33:10	14:60[c]	151[c]
33:12	14:120	182
33:14	14:288	254
33:18	14:60[c]	151[c]
33:19	14:104	176
33:20	14:30, 248	133, 237
33:23	14:30	133
34:6	14:56	150
34:12	17:404	801
34:15	15:152, 166; 17:404[c]	369, 376, 801[c]
34:16	15:152, 166	369, 376
34:21	17:168	705
34:27	16:250	575
35:2	17:168	705
35:3	17:168	705

Leviticus

3:17	16:368[c]	627[c]
5:1	17:326	771
5:2	15:40, 202	318, 394
5:4	17:128	688
5:5	17:128	688
5:6	17:128	688
6:5	17:332 [5:21]	773–774 [5:21]
6:6[o]	17:332[x]	773–774[x]
7:18	15:40	318
7:20	15:40	318
7:23	16:160[c]	540[c]
10:1	17:74[c]	666[c]
10:2	17:74[c]	666[c]
11:44	17:170	706
16:8	17:132	690
16:29	17:106	679
17:11	16:160	540
18	15:152	369
18:5	16:106, 132[c]	518, 529[c]
18:6	17:290[c]	756[c]
18:12	17:292	757
18:16[o]	15:128	359

18:18	15:126, 128, 130[1]	358, 359, 360[2]
18:20	17:290	756
18:22	17:218	727
18:23	17:218[c]	727[c]
19:3	17:356	784
19:9	17:342–344	779
19:11	17:302–304, 330[c], 332	762, 773 (twice)[3]
19:12	17:126	687
19:13	17:336	775
19:14	17:264	745
19:15	17:384	794
19:16	17:312	766
19:17	17:326	771
19:18	16:144[c]; 17:196, 254, 288	532[c], 717, 741, 755
19:20	17:368	787
19:26	17:148	696
19:28	15:230	405
19:29	17:290	756
19:31	17:148	696
19:32	17:360	785
19:33	17:382[c]	793[c]
19:34	17:382[c]	793[c]
19:35	17:334	775
19:36	17:334	774
20:6	17:148	696
20:9	17:358[c]	784[c]
20:11	17:290	756
20:18	17:292	757
20:27	17:148	696
21:1	15:230	405
21:2	17:262[c]	744[c]
21:4	17:262	744
21:5	17:262	744
21:11	15:230	405
23:3	17:168–170	705
24:8	16:368[c]	627[c]
24:11	17:154	698
24:14	17:154	698
24:19	17:286	755
24:20	17:286[c]	755[c]
25:14	17:334	774–775
25:20	15:64	329
25:21	15:64	329
25:23	17:340[c]	777[c]
25:35	17:338, 340[c], 344, 374	775–776, 777[c], 779, 790

25:36	17:338, 340[c]	775–776, 777[c]
25:37	17:338[c], 340[c]	775[c], 777[c]
25:39	17:368[c]	788[c]
25:40	17:368[c]	788[c]
25:44	17:368	787
25:45	17:368[c]	787[c]
25:46	17:368[c]	787[c]
26	16:106; 17:412	518, 804
26:1	17:134[c]	691[c]
26:31	17:76	667
26:39	15:186	385
26:40	15:188	386

Numbers

5:12	17:292[c]	756[c]
5:21	17:132	689
6	17:114	681
9:10	16:210	559
9:11	16:210	559
11:2	17:276	750
11:11	17:384	794
11:16	17:388	795
11:17	14:362; 17:388[c]	283, 795[c]
11:18	15:374; 17:102	464, 677
11:20[o]	17:102[x]	677[x]
11:25	14:362; 17:388[c]	283, 795[c]
11:26	14:362	283
11:28	17:266[c]	746[c]
11:29	14:362	283
12:1	15:146	366
12:2	17:244	736
12:3	17:284	754
14:1	17:54	658
14:13	17:384	794
14:15	17:52	657
14:16	17:52	657
14:19	17:276	750
14:20	17:276	750
14:24	14:360	283
14:33	15:184	385
14:44	17:54	658
15:30	17:54, 158, 160	658, 700 (twice)
15:32	17:170	705

15:39	17:32	649
16:1	17:402	800
16:3	17:244	736
16:15	17:330	773
16:22	15:32, 50–52	312, 324
16:27	15:184	385
16:32	15:184	385
18:8	16:368[c]	627[c]
20:10	15:364; 17:54	460, 658
20:11	15:364[c]; 17:54	460[c], 658
20:12	17:166[c]	702[c]
21:5	14:360	282
22:12	17:134	690
22:20	14:280[c]; 17:134	252[c], 690
22:22	14:280	251
22:31	14:280	251–252
22:32	14:280	252
22:34	14:280	252
22:35	14:280	252
23:8	14:280[1]; 17:104 [23:12]	252[2], 677 [23:12]
23:9	15:228	404
23:10	15:228[23:14], 358	404 [23:14], 458
23:19[o]	14:34 [23:23]	135
23:20[3]	14:280	252
23:23	17:148 [23:27]	696 [23:27]
25:7	17:152[c]	697[c]
25:11	16:38–40[c]	490–491[c]
25:12	16:38–40[c]	490–491[c]
27:16	15:32	312–313
27:18	16:214[c]	560–561[c]
30:2	17:116	682
30:13	17:114	681–682
31:16	16:314–316	605
31:27	17:410	803
33:52	17:140	692
34:[o]	17:406	802
35:15[o]	17:406[c]	802[c]
35:31	17:286	754
35:34	17:286	754

Deuteronomy

1:9	17:384	794
1:13	17:388–390	795–796
2:30	15:70	331

3:25	17:100	676
3:26	17:100	676
4	17:412	804
4:2	16:280	591
4:6	17:26	647
4:9	17:354	783
4:15	17:136–138, 138^{c}	691, 692^{c}
4:16	17:136–138, 138^{c}	691, 692^{c}
4:29	15:380	467
4:30	15:380^{c}	467^{c}
4:31	15:380^{c}	467^{c}
4:33	14:248	237
4:35	14:48	146–147
4:37	14:98	172
4:39	14:48	147
4:45°	16:104 [5:2]	517 [5:2]
5:5	15:286	431
5:12	17:172	706
5:14	17:172	706
5:15	17:174	706–707
5:26°	14:246 [5:32]	236 [5:32]
5:32°	17:72 [5:38]	664 [5:38]
6:4	14:48, 52, 198, 282^{q}; 17:50 [6:5]	147, 148, 214, 252^{q}, 656 [6:5]
6:5	16:144^{c}; 17:52	532^{c}, 657
6:6	17:354	783
6:7	17:354	783
6:13	17:118–120	684
6:24	16:106^{c}, 110	518^{c}, 520
6:25	16:106, 110	518, 520
7:3	15:152 (twice), 166	368, 369, 376
7:4	15:152, 166; 17:404	369, 376, 801
7:5	17:140^{c}	692^{c}
7:6	14:98, 110^{c}	172, 178^{c}
7:7	14:98^{c}, 110^{c}	172^{c}, 178^{c}
7:8	14:98^{c}, 110^{c}	172^{c}, 178^{c}
7:9	14:110	178
7:12	14:110–112	178
7:25	17:140^{c}	692^{c}
8:2	15:82	338
8:3	15:58, 64	327, 329
8:4	15:64	329
9:5	14:130, 152–154	186, 195
10:12	17:50	657
12:13	17:50	657
10:16	16:166	543

10:18	17:376, 382[c]	790, 793[c]
10:19	17:382[c]	793[c]
10:20	17:120[c]	684[c]
11:18	16:256	577–578
11:19	16:256[c]	577–578[c]
11:20	16:256	577–578
12:2	17:140[c]	692[c]
12:3	17:140[c]	692[c]
12:7	17:204	721
12:12	17:204[c]	721[c]
12:18	17:204[c]	721[c]
12:30	17:76	667
12:31	17:76	667
12:32	17:72	665
13:1	16:222	564
13:2	16:222	564
13:3	16:222	564
13:6	17:258–260, 274	743, 750
13:7	17:258[c]	743[c]
13:8	17:258[c]	743[c]
14:1	16:52[c]; 17:170–172, 262	496[c], 706, 744
14:28	17:376	790
14:29	17:376	790
15:2	17:372	789
15:4	17:412[c]	804[c]
15:5	17:412[c]	804[c]
15:6[1]	17:412 (twice)	804 (twice)
15:7	17:336, 374	775, 790
15:8[o]	17:336[x]	775[x]
15:11	17:372	789
15:12	17:368[c]	788[c]
15:13	17:368[c]	788[c]
15:16	17:368[c]	788[c]
15:17	17:368[c]	788[c]
16:21	17:134	691
16:22	17:134–136	691
17:16[o]	15:138	363
17:17	15:130 (twice)[2], 136	359, 360 (twice)[3], 363
17:19	16:254[c]	577[c]
17:20	17:384	794
18:10	17:148	696
18:11	17:148–150	696
18:12	17:148–150	696
18:13	16:46; 17:38	493, 652
18:15	14:290; 15:258, 288; 16:116[c]	255, 418, 432, 523[c]

18:16[o]	14:290; 15:258[4]	255, 418[5]
19:16	17:310	765
19:19[o]	17:310[x]	765[x]
20:1	17:408	802
20:14	17:410	803
20:19	17:406	802
21:1	17:286	754–755
21:13	15:162	374
21:14	15:158, 162	372, 374
21:18	17:354, 358	783, 784
21:19	17:354[c]	783[c]
21:20	17:354[c]	783[c]
21:23	15:304	439
22:1	17:260	743
22:5	17:222	728
22:6	17:268	747
22:7	17:268[c]	747[c]
22:8	17:268[c]	747[c]
22:14	17:352	783
22:17	17:324	770
22:19	15:168	376
22:20	15:152; 17:352	368, 783
22:21	15:152; 17:290–292	368, 756
22:22[o]	17:290–292[x]	756[x]
22:23	15:152; 17:290–292	368, 756
22:28	17:290[c]	756[c]
22:29	15:168	376
23:2	15:122; 17:292	356, 756
23:7	17:382	792
23:8	17:382[c]	792[c]
23:9	17:406	802
23:15	17:406[c]	802[c]
23:17	17:218, 290 (twice)	727, 756 (twice)
23:19	17:338, 342[c]	776, 777[c]
23:20	17:340[c]	776[c]
23:21	17:114–116	682
23:24	17:330	773
23:25	17:330[c]	773[c]
24:1	15:158 (twice), 162, 170	372 (twice), 374, 378
24:6	17:342	778
24:7	17:334	774
24:10	17:342	778
24:14	17:336	775
24:15	17:336[c]	775[c]
24:19	17:372	789

24:20	17:372[c]	789[c]
24:21	17:372[c]	789[c]
25:3	17:388	795
25:11	17:220	727
25:12	17:220[c]	727[c]
25:13	17:334	775
25:14	17:334[c]	775[c]
25:15	17:334[c]	775[c]
25:17	17:288	755
26:5	17:362	786
26:11	17:204	721
26:15	15:28	311
26:17	17:412[c]	804[c]
26:18	17:412[c]	804[c]
26:19	17:412[c]	804[c]
27	15:152	369
27:13[6]	17:98	675
27:15	17:136	691
27:16	17:358	784
27:18	17:264	745
27:19	17:376, 382	790, 793
27:20	17:292	756
27:21	17:218	727
27:22	17:292	757
27:24	17:286	755
27:25	17:286	754
27:26	16:106, 132[c]	518, 529[c]
28:1	17:412[c]	804[c]
28:14	17:72[c]	664[c]
28:15	15:84	337
28:22	15:214–216	399
28:28	15:70, 84	331, 337
28:47	17:44	654
28:48	17:114	681
28:58	17:60	660
29	17:412	804
29:1	16:322	607–608
29:2	16:224	565
29:3	16:224[c]	565[c]
29:4	14:150; 16:224	194, 565
29:5	15:64	329
29:29	14:36; 16:256; 17:32–34	136, 578, 650
30:1	15:360	459
30:6	15:374; 16:166	464, 543
30:11	16:256	578

30:19	15:210	396
31:9	16:256	577
31:10	16:256	577
31:11	16:256	577
31:13	16:222	564
31:16	14:56, 86 (twice)[7]	150, 165 (twice)[8]
31:17	14:86[c]	165[c]
31:18	14:86	165
31:19	14:86[9], 16:250	165[c], 575
31:20	14:56, 86	150, 166
31:21	14:56, 86, 122	150, 166, 182
31:27	14:86[c]	165[c]
32:4	14:58; 15:60	151, 328
32:18	14:246[c]	236[c]
32:27	14:34	135
32:29	17:406	802
32:30	17:406	802
32:35	17:288	755
32:39	14:48	147
32:40	14:54; 17:120	149, 684
33:2	15:34, 100	315, 345

Joshua

1:6	17:246[c]	738[c]
1:7	17:72[c], 246[c]	665[c], 738[c]
1:8	16:254[c]	577[c]
1:9	17:246–248	738
1:17	17:400	800
2[o,1]	16:38	490
2:4	17:308[c]	764[c] [2:45]
2:5	17:308[c]	764[c] [2:45]
4:7	16:368[c]	627[c]
5:4	16:52, 210	496, 559
5:14	14:280; 15:36 [6:2], 104 [6:2]	252, 315 [6:2], 347 [6:2]
5:15[o]	15:104 [6:2]	347 [6:2]
6:2	14:280	252
6:21	15:184	385
7:[o]	15:190	387
7:1	15:190	387
7:9	17:52	657
7:11	15:190; 17:116	387, 682
7:14	17:132	690
7:19	15:384; 17:130	468, 689

7:21	17:228	730
7:24	15:184	385
7:25	15:184	385
9:19	17:120–122	685
11:20	15:70	331
22:7[o]	17:410[x]	803[x]
22:8	17:410	803
24:2	15:350	455
24:3	15:350	455–456
24:15	17:394	797
24:19	14:56, 246	150, 236
24:22	17:110	680
24:23	17:110[c]	680[c]
24:32	17:262[c]	745[c]

Judges

2	17:412	804
2:1	14:292	256
2:18	14:32	134
3	17:412	804
3:19	17:308[c]	764[c]
3:20	17:24[c], 308[c]	646[c], 764[c]
4:4	16:244[c]	572[c]
4:18	17:308[c]	764[c]
4:19	17:308[c]	764[c]
5:7	17:236	734
5:23	17:98	675
6:11	14:280	252
6:12	14:280	252
6:14	14:280 (twice)	252 (twice)
6:16	14:280	252
6:17	14:282	252
6:20	14:280	252
6:21	14:250, 280	237, 252
6:22	14:280	252
6:23	14:280	252
8:23	17:242[c]	735[c]
8:30	15:148	366
8:31	15:148	366
9:1	17:244	736
9:2	17:244	736
9:23	15:68	331
10:16	14:34	135
11:3[o]	17:278 [11:5]	751 [11:5]

13:18	14:60	152
13:21	14:244[c], 250[c]	234[c], 237[c]
13:22	14:244[1], 250[c]	234[2], 237[c]
15:19	15:238	408
16:23	14:244[c]	234[c]
17:4	17:138	692
17:13	17:138	692
19:2	15:172	378
19:22	17:290[c]	756[c]
21:7	17:122	685

Ruth

1:17	17:118	684
1:21	14:46	145
2:4	17:362, 364	785, 786
2:7	17:364	786
2:10	17:294	758

1 Samuel

1:11	17:110	680
1:13	17:86, 92[1]	671, 674[2]
1:14	17:310	765
1:26	17:130	688–689
2	17:354	783
2:2	14:56	150
2:10	15:148	366
2:25	15:82	337
2:29	17:152[c], 258	697[c], 743
2:30	14:66	155
2:31	15:184	385
2:33	15:184	385
2:36	15:184	385
3:13	17:152[c]	697[c]
3:15	17:326	771
3:21	14:282	252
4:3	17:76	667
6:19	17:34	650
6:20	14:56	150
7:5	17:106[c]	679[c]
7:6	17:106	679
7:10[o]	17:406 [7:9]	802 [7:9]
10:1	17:242	735
10:20	17:132	690

10:21	17:246	737
10:22	17:246	737
10:24	14:98	172
11:15[o]	17:390 [12:2]	796 [12:2]
12:1[o]	17:390 [12:3]	796 [12:3]
12:3	17:330	773
13:12	17:74	666–667
13:13	14:66; 17:74, 324	155, 666–667, 770
13:14	14:66	155
14:6	17:408	802
14:28[o]	17:406 [14:29]	802 [14:29]
14:39[o]	17:128 [14:40]	688 [14:40]
14:44[o]	17:128 [14:45], 356 [14:45]	688 [14:45], 783 [14:45]
14:45	17:400	799
15:2	15:186	386
15:3	15:186	386
15:6	17:276	750
15:11	17:100	676
15:15	17:74	667
15:16	17:74	667
15:22	17:68	663–664
15:23	17:70	664
15:24	15:358	458
15:29	14:34[c]	135[c]
15:33	15:186; 17:406–408	386, 802
16:1[o]	17:258 [16:2]	743 [16:2]
16:7	14:134; 17:204	187, 720
16:8	17:204[c]	720[c]
16:14	15:70	331
16:15	15:108	348
17:47	17:408	802–803
18:7	17:266[c]	746[c]
18:8	17:266[c]	746[c]
19	17:24	646
19:20	17:360	785
20:2[o]	17:400	799
20:6	17:308[c]	764[c]
20:28	17:308[c]	764[c]
20:32	17:356	784
21:3	17:300[c]	761[c]
21:6	16:52[c]	496[c]
22:2	17:278	751
22:8	17:310–312	765
22:9	17:312	766
22:17	17:400	800

22:18	17:402	800
23:22	17:406	802
24:9[o]	17:312 [24:10]	766 [24:10]
24:11	15:40	318
25:1	17:262[c]	745[c]
25:3	17:230	731
25:11	17:230	731
25:17	17:322	769
25:22	17:128[c]	688[c]
25:33	17:128[c]	688[c]
25:34	17:128[c]	688[c]
25:42	15:148	367
25:43	15:148	367
27:1	17:58	659
30:12	15:238	408
30:22	17:278	751
30:24	17:410	803
31:13	17:106–108	679

2 Samuel

1:12	17:260	744
1:24	17:234	733
2:4	17:390	796
3:24[o]	17:266–268	747
3:27[o]	17:266–268	747
3:31[o]	17:260[c]	744[c]
3:32[o]	17:260	744
5:12	15:148	367
5:13	15:148	367
6:20	17:352	782
7:13	14:44	143
7:18	17:90, 92[1]	672, 674[2]
7:19	14:44	144
9:1	17:346	780
10:3	17:312	765
12:8	15:138–140	363–364
12:11	15:66, 68, 78 (twice)[3]	330, 331, 334, 335[4]
12:12	15:68, 78	331, 334
12:14	17:166[c]	703[c]
12:16	17:90, 100, 106	672, 676, 678
12:17	17:100[c]	676[c]
12:18	17:100[c]	676[c]
14:20	15:34	314
15:2	17:244	736

15:3	17:322[c]	769[c]
15:4	17:244, 322[c]	736, 769[c]
16:3	15:244	412
16:10	15:68; 17:66	331, 663
17:23	17:200[c]	719[c]
19:23[o]	17:130 [19:24]	688 [19:24]
19:33[o]	17:346 [19:34]	780 [19:34]
20:1	17:402	800
21:1	15:184; 17:152 [21:2]	385, 698 [21:2]
21:2	17:152–154 [21:3]	698 [21:3]
21:11	17:12	641
21:12	17:12[c]	641[c]
21:17	17:398	799
22:28	17:246	736
22:42	17:84	671
23:2	16:248	574
23:17	16:198	555
24:[o,5]	15:74–76	333–334
24:1	15:68, 78	331, 334
24:10	15:384	468
24:16	15:102	346
24:17	15:188	386–387

1 Kings

1:4	15:140	364
1:6	17:354	783
2:3	17:384	794
2:5	17:286	755
2:6	17:286[c]	755[c]
2:7	17:346	780
2:8	17:130	688
2:9	17:130	688
2:19	17:356	784
2:23	17:118[c]	684[c]
2:24	17:118[c]	684[c]
2:26	17:388	795
2:33	17:286	755
2:34	17:286[c]	755[c]
2:36	17:130[c]	688[c]
2:37	17:130[c]	688[c]
2:42	17:130[c]	688[c]
3:3	17:78–80	668
3:8	17:384[c]	794[c]
3:9	17:384	794

3:10	17:384[c]	794[c]
3:11	17:82	669–670
3:12	17:82	669–670
5:12	17:404[c]	801[c]
8:1	14:284	253
8:10	14:60	152
8:11	14:60[c]	152[c]
8:21	16:104	517
8:22	17:90	672
8:27	14:42; 15:28	142–143, 311
8:30	15:28	311
8:48	15:382	467
8:54	17:90	672–673
8:60	14:48	147
11:1	15:138[1], 150, 154	363[2], 367, 370
11:33	14:244[c]	234[c]
12:31	17:74	667
12:32	17:74[c]	667[c]
13:15	17:264	746
13:16	17:264[c]	746[c]
13:22	17:70[c]	664[c]
14:24	17:218	727
15:5	15:142	365
15:11	15:142	365
15:12	17:290	756
15:14	15:142; 16:22	365, 483
15:19	17:404[c]	801[c]
17:[o,3]	17:382	792
17:4	15:64	329
17:12	14:38	138
17:14	15:64	329
17:21	15:238	408
17:24	15:94	341
18:12	17:240[c]	734[c]
18:13	17:240	734–735
18:17	17:32	649
18:27	17:300, 322	761, 770
18:28	17:252	740
19:3	16:316[c]; 17:208	605[c], 722
19:4	17:68, 100	663, 676
19:10	16:234; 17:152[c]	568, 697[c]
19:11	14:60	151–152
19:14	16:234	568
19:18	16:234	568
19:21	17:360	785

20:16	17:214[c]	725[c]
20:34[o,4]	17:270	748
20:35	17:72, 270[5]	665, 748[6]
20:36[o,7]	17:270	748
20:42[o,8]	17:270	748
21:7	17:392	796–797
21:25	15:154	370
21:27	17:108[c]	679[c]
21:28	17:108[c]	679[c]
21:29	17:108	679
22:15	17:300	761
22:19	14:60, 250; 15:100	152, 237, 345
22:20	15:68–70	331
22:21	15:34, 108	314, 348
22:22	14:386; 15:70	292, 331
22:46[o]	17:290 [22:47]	756 [22:47]

2 Kings

1:2	17:56	659
2:2	17:360	785
2:4	17:360	785
2:6	17:360	785
2:9	14:362	283
2:11	16:336[c]	614[c]
2:15	14:362; 17:364	283, 786
2:23	17:362	785
2:24	17:98, 362[c]	675, 785[c]
2:25	17:362[c]	785[c]
4:[o,1]	17:382	792
4:1	17:368	787
4:15	17:220	727–728
5:12	15:364	460
5:15	17:242[c]	735[c]
5:16	17:242	735–736
5:17	17:144[c]	694[c]
5:18	17:144[c]	694[c]
5:19	17:144[c]	694[c]
5:20	17:370	788
6:2	16:302[c]	600[c]
6:17	15:104	347
6:32	17:324[c]	770[c]
7:2[o]	17:54 [6:35]	658 [6:35]
7:9[o]	17:322 [7:7]	769 [7:7]

8	15:154	370
8:12	14:56, 82[c]	150, 164[c]
9:30	17:222	728
10:16	17:154	698
11:4	17:358	784
12:2[o]	17:358 [12:3]	785 [12:3]
14:8	17:250	739
16:1	16:264[c]	583[c]
16:2	16:264	583
16:7	17:404[c]	801[c]
16:10	17:74	667
17:2	15:186	386
17:3	15:186	386
17:4	15:186; 17:126	386, 687
17:13	14:148	193
17:14	14:148[x]; 15:186	193[x], 385–386
17:28	17:138	692
17:33	17:62	661
18:2	16:264[c]	583[c]
18:4	17:140	693
18:7	17:126	687
19:6	17:154	698
19:15	14:48	147
19:27	14:122	182
19:35	15:34, 104	315, 346–347
20:[o,2]	15:90–92	340
20:1	14:66[c]	155[c]
20:13	17:226	730
20:14	17:226[c]	730[c]
21:6	17:150	696
22:19	15:378	466
23	17:140	692
23:26	15:186	386
24:3[o]	15:188 [24:5]	386 [24:5]
24:8[o]	16:264 [24:10]	583 [24:10]

1 Chronicles

2:46	15:148	367
2:48	15:148	367
7:1	15:148	367
7:4	15:148	367
7:14	15:148	367
13:2	17:384–386	794
15:13	17:74	667

15:15	17:74	667
17:12	14:44[c]	144[c]
17:14	14:44[c]	144[c]
17:17	14:44[c]	144[c]
17:25	17:100	676
17:26	17:100[c]	676[c]
21:[o,1]	15:74–76	333–334
21:1	15:68, 78, 110	331, 334, 350
21:15	14:282	252
21:16	14:282; 15:102–104	252, 346
21:17	14:282	252
21:18	14:282	252
21:19	14:282	252
26:13	17:132–134	690
26:14	17:132[c]	690[c]
28:2	17:386	794
28:5	15:150	367
28:6	14:112; 16:50	178, 495
28:7	14:112	178–179
28:9	14:54, 112	149, 179
29:2	17:346	779
29:3[o]	17:346[x]	779[x]
29:14	17:64	661–662

2 Chronicles

1:10	17:384[c]	794[c]
2:4	17:176[c]	708[c]
6:12	17:90[c]	673[c]
6:13	17:90[c]	673[c]
6:16	14:112	179
6:30	14:54	149
8:13	17:178[c]	708[c]
10:15	15:64	330
11:15	17:140	692
11:17	15:150	367
11:21	15:150	367
12:9	17:76	667
14:3	17:140[c]	692[c]
14:11	17:408	803
15:1	14:112[c]	179[c]
15:2	14:112; 16:78	179, 506
15:8	17:140[c]	692[c]
15:12	15:214; 17:110	398, 680
15:13	17:110[c]	680[c]

15:14	15:214; 17:110	398, 680
15:17	16:22	483
16:3	17:406[c]	802[c]
16:7	17:56, 324[c], 404[c]	658, 770–771[c], 801[c]
16:9	15:56	327
16:12	17:56	658
16:14	17:262	744–745
17:9	16:262	582
17:10	16:262[c]	582[c]
18:1	17:404[c]	801[c]
18:5	17:416	805
19:2	17:258, 404[c]	743, 801[c]
19:6	17:386	794
20:3	17:208	722
20:5	17:90	673
20:6	14:46	145
20:13	17:90	673
20:20	14:332; 17:52	271, 657
20:21	17:408	803
21:4	17:364–366	786
21:10	17:400	800
21:13	17:366	786
23:17	17:140[c]	693[c]
24:2	15:142	365
24:3	15:142	365
24:4	17:76[c]	667[c]
24:5[o]	17:76[c]	667[c]
24:6	17:76[c]	667[c]
24:17	17:392	796
24:20	17:324[c]	771[c]
24:24	17:408	803
25:7	17:404[c]	801[c]
25:8	17:404[c]	801[c]
25:16	17:328	772
26:18	17:400	800
28:6	17:164	702
29:6	16:282	591
30:2	16:210[c]	559[c]
30:3	16:210[c]	559[c]
30:6	15:360	459
30:9	15:380	467
30:13	16:208[c]	558–559[c]
30:14	16:208	558–559
30:15	16:208	558–559
30:18	17:80	668

30:19	17:80	668
30:20	17:80	668
30:22	15:384	468
31:1	17:140[c]	693[c]
31:3	17:178[c]	708[c]
32:31	15:88	338
33:8	14:112[c]	179[c]
34:3	17:360	785
34:4	17:140[c]	692–693[c]
34:30	16:256	578
35:20	17:250[c]	739[c]
35:21	17:250	739
35:22	14:66[c]; 17:250	155[c], 739
36:7	17:76	667
36:9	16:264; 17:362	583, 785
36:13	15:84; 17:126, 128[c], 406[c]	337, 687 (twice)[1], 802[c]
36:15	14:148[c], 166	193[c], 200
36:16	14:148, 166–168	193, 200
36:20	17:170	705
36:21	17:170	705

Ezra

1:7	17:76[c]	667[c]
2:68	17:346	780
2:69	17:346	780
4:12	16:316	605
6:17	16:344	618
6:21	16:208	559
8:21	17:108	679
9:3	17:108[c]	679[c]
10:3	15:158[c], 166	372[c], 376
10:5	17:110, 132	680, 689
10:11	15:152	369

Nehemiah

1:4	17:106	678
2:2	17:208	722
2:5	17:242	735
2:19	16:316[c]	605[c]
4:4	17:98	675
5:8	17:332	774
5:14	17:240[c], 386	735[c], 795
5:15	17:240	735

6:6	16:316	605
6:11	17:250	739
6:12	17:416	805
6:14	17:98	675
8:8	16:262	582[1]
8:9	16:262	582[2]
9:2	15:188, 384; 16:256[c]	386, 468, 578[c]
9:3	16:256	578
9:6	15:4, 28, 54, 58, 100	300, 311, 326, 327, 345
9:13	15:118–120	354
9:14	15:118–120	354–355
9:20	14:360	283
9:30	14:360	283
10:29[o]	17:110 [10:30]	680 [10:30]
10:31[o]	17:170 [10:32]	705 [10:32]
10:34[o]	17:134 [10:35]	690 [10:35]
13:15	17:170	705
13:22	17:22	645
13:23	15:152, 158[c], 166	369, 372[c], 376
13:25	17:98, 132	675, 689
13:26	15:150	367
13:30	15:152, 158[c], 166	369, 372[c], 376

Esther

1:8	17:214	724–725
1:22	17:350	782
2:12	15:140	364
2:13	15:140	364
2:15	17:204	720
3:2	17:400	800
3:3	17:400[c]	800[c]
3:4	17:400[c]	800[c]
3:6	17:392	797
3:8	16:316	605
3:9	17:392	797
4:3	17:108	679
4:15	17:108	679
4:16	17:108	679
9:13	17:288	756
9:31	17:108	679
9:32	17:108[c]	679[c]

Job

1	15:110	349
1:5	15:348; 17:234	455, 732
1:6	15:34, 100, 108, 110	315, 345, 348, 350
1:7	15:108	348
1:11	17:102	677
1:12	15:108; 17:102	349, 677
1:21	17:118	683
1:22	17:66	662
2	15:110	349
2:1	15:100, 108	345, 348
2:5	17:102[c]	677[c]
2:6	17:102[c]	677[c]
2:9	17:352	782
2:10	17:66	662–663
3:2	17:68, 102[c]	663, 677[c]
3:3	17:102	677
3:16[o,1]	15:220	401
4	15:390	470
4:18	15:36, 98	315, 344
5:1	17:146	695
5:3	17:62	660–661
5:7	15:60, 214	328, 399
5:12	17:34	650
5:15	17:332	774
5:17	15:386	469 [5:7]
5:21	17:312–314	766
7:11	17:68	663
7:20	15:58	327
9:8	15:4	300
9:10	15:58	328
9:20	15:192	388
9:22	15:390[c]	470[c]
9:23	15:390[c]	470[c]
10:8	15:48	323
10:9	15:48	323
10:10	15:48	323
10:15	15:192	388
10:21	15:220	401
11:7	14:54	149
11:8	14:42, 54[c]	143, 149[c]
11:9	14:42[2], 54[c]	143[3], 149[c]
11:13	15:360	459
12:1	17:236[c]	734[c]

12:3	17:236[x], 324	734[x], 770
12:6	15:60	328
12:9	14:24	130
12:18	17:388	795
12:21	17:362	786
12:24	17:34	650
12:25	17:34[c]	650[c]
13:2	17:236	734
13:7	17:298	759
13:15	17:40, 56	653, 659
14:4	15:194	389
14:5	15:58 [14:6], 90	328 [14:6], 339
14:10[o]	15:220 [14:11]	401 [14:11]
14:12[o]	15:220 [14:13]; 16:368 [14:13]	401 [14:13], 628 [14:13]
15:14	15:194	389
15:15	14:56; 15:36, 98	150, 315, 344
15:25	17:64	662
15:26	17:64[c]	662[c]
15:27	17:64[c]	662[c]
17:13[o]	15:220 [17:12]	401 [17:12]
17:15	15:220 [17:14]	401 [17:14]
17:16[o]	15:220 [17:15]	401 [17:15]
19:3	17:294	759
19:7	17:68 [19:6]	663 [19:6]
19:13	17:276	751
19:25	15:258; 16:348	418, 619
19:26	15:258; 16:348, 352	418, 619, 621
19:27	16:352	621
20:4	14:44	143
20:11	17:360	785
20:15	17:228	730
20:18	17:332[c]	774[c]
20:19	17:332	774
21:7	15:60	328
22:2	17:22	645
22:19	17:204	721
23:3	17:40	653
24:23	15:60; 17:62	328, 661
25:3	15:34	315
25:5	15:36	315
26:6	14:54	149
26:7	15:36	315
26:13	14:360; 15:14	282, 305
27:3	14:360	282
27:5	17:38	652

27:6	17:38[c]	652[c]
28:13	17:34	650
28:14	17:34	650
28:15	17:30	648
28:20	15:12	304
28:21	15:12[c]	304[c]
28:22	15:12[c]	304[c]
28:23	15:12[c]	304[c]
28:24	15:12[c]	304[c]
28:25	15:12[c]	304[c]
28:26	15:12[c]	304[c]
28:27	15:12	304
28:28	17:28	648
29:8	17:236	734
29:11	17:24, 376, 378[4]	646, 790, 791[5]
29:12[6]	17:378	791
30	15:390	470
30:1	17:244[c]	736[c]
30:25	17:268	747
31:1	17:220	727
31:4	15:56	327
31:5	17:40[c]	653[c]
31:6	17:40	653
31:9	17:290	756
31:10	17:290[c]	756[c]
31:13	17:366	787
31:15	15:48	323
31:16	17:376	790
31:17[o]	17:376[x]	790[x]
31:32	17:382	792
31:35	17:40	653
32:4	17:360	785
32:6	17:360	785
32:8	15:38	317
32:21	17:314–316	767
32:22	17:314[c]	767[c]
33:4	14:360	282
33:18	15:228–230	404
34:14	15:236	407
34:15	15:236	407
34:21	15:62	329
34:22	17:62	661
35:7	17:22	645
36:14	15:230	404
36:26	14:42 (twice)	143 (twice)

38	15:36	315
38:7	15:32, 34, 100	313, 315, 345
38:12	15:92	341
38:33	15:92–94	341
40:19[o]	15:12 [40:14]	304
42:2	14:46	145
42:11	17:242[c]	735[c]

Psalms

1:1	17:278	751
1:2	17:44	654
1:6	14:120	182
2	15:284, 314[1]	430, 443[2]
2:6	14:184; 15:296 (twice)	207, 435 (twice)
2:7	14:88, 182, 184, 244[c], 318, 348	166, 206, 207, 235[c], 266, 277
2:8	14:348; 16:360[c]	277, 624[c]
2:9	15:300; 16:360[c]	437, 624[c]
2:11	14:348; 17:60	277, 660
2:12	14:348	277
3:2[o]	15:390 [3:3]	470 [3:3]
3:6[o]	17:248 [3:7]	738 [3:7]
3:8[o]	17:96 [3:9]	674 [3:9]
4:6	17:204	721
4:7	17:204	721
4:8	17:204[c]	721[c]
5:3[o]	17:94 [5:4]	674 [5:4]
5:4	14:56 [5:5]; 15:72[3]	150, 332[4]
5:6	17:296 [5:7], 318 [5:7]	759 [5:7], 767 [5:7]
5:10[o]	17:98 [5:11]	675 [5:11]
6:5	15:220	401
7:6	15:40	318
7:10[5]	14:52	148
7:14	15:198	391
8:5[o]	14:244 [8:6]	234 [8:6]
8:6	15:34	315
10:3	17:24	646
10:5	17:62	661
10:6	17:62[c]	661[c]
12:1[o]	17:296 [12:2]	759 [12:2]
12:2[6]	17:296, 316, 318	759, 767 (twice)
12:3	17:322 [12:4]	769 [12:4]
14:1	14:24; 17:24, 50	130, 646, 656
14:6	17:56	658

15:1	17:10	641
15:2	17:10[c], 296, 330	641[c], 759, 773
15:4	17:122, 244, 318	685, 736, 768
15:5	17:342	777
16:10	15:230; 16:348	405, 619
16:11	14:60; 15:28; 16:374	151, 311, 630
17:14	15:390; 16:348	470, 619
17:15	16:348[x], 374	619[x], 630
18:2	17:52	657
18:3	17:52[c]	657[c]
18:7[o]	14:60[c] [18:8]	152[c] [18:8]
18:19[o]	16:44[x]	493[x]
18:20[o]	16:44 [18:21]	492 [18:21]
18:23[o]	16:44 [18:24]	493 [18:24]
18:24	16:44 [18:25]	492 [18:25]
18:31[o,7]	14:52 [18:32]	149 [18:32]
18:32	17:248[c]	738[c]
18:37[o]	17:288 [18:38]	755 [18:38]
18:41[o]	17:408 [18:42]	802 [18:42]
18:42	17:288[8], 408 [18:43]	755[9], 802 [18:43]
19:1[o]	14:24 [19:2]; 15:14 [19:2, 3], 208 [19:2]	130 [19:2], 305 [19:2, 3], 396 [19:2]
19:7[o]	14:58 [19:8]; 16:258 [19:8]	151 [19:8], 579 [19:8]
19:9[o]	15:60 [19:10]; 16:266 [19:10]	328 [19:10], 585 [19:10]
19:13	16:46; 17:48 [19:14]	493, 655 [19:14]
19:14[10]	15:294	434–435
22	15:304	439
22:20[o]	15:230 [22:21]	404 [22:21]
23:1	17:224	729
23:2	17:224[c]	729[c]
23:4	17:248	738
23:5	17:234	732
24:4	17:282	754
25:6	14:56	150
25:7	17:360	785
25:9	17:284	754
25:14	14:24; 17:28	129, 648
25:22	17:96	674
26:1	16:76; 17:38	505, 652
26:2	15:88	339
26:4	17:278	751
26:5	17:278[c]	751[c]
26:6	17:282	754
26:10	17:390	796
27	17:52	658

27:1	17:250	739
27:14	17:56	659
28:3	17:318	767–768
28:7	17:52–54[c]	658[c]
28:9	17:96[c]	674[c]
29:10	15:58	328
30:6[o]	17:62 [30:7]	661 [30:7]
30:7	15:58 [30:8]	327 [30:8]
30:11[o]	17:204 [30:12]	721 [30:12]
30:12	17:204[c] [30:13]	721[c] [30:13]
31:5[o]	15:246 [31:6]	412 [31:6]
31:6	17:258 [31:7]	743 [31:7]
31:24[o]	17:56 [31:25]	659 [31:25]
32:5	15:384	468
32:10	17:54[c]	658[c]
33:6	15:6, 14, 36; 17:86	301, 305, 316, 671
33:9	14:46; 15:6, 36	145, 301, 316
33:11	14:74	161
33:12	17:412	804
33:14	15:56[c]	327[c]
33:15	14:54; 15:48	149, 323
33:16	17:408	803
33:17	17:408[c]	803[c]
34:7[o]	15:100 [34:8]	346 [34:8]
34:9	17:224–226	729
34:10	17:224–226[x]	729[x]
34:11	17:60 [34:12]	660 [34:12]
34:12	17:314[c]	766[c]
34:13	17:314	766
34:14	15:382 [34:15]	462 [34:15]
34:18[o,11]	15:390	470
34:19[12]	15:390	470
35:13	17:106	678
36:6[o]	14:58 [36:7]	151
37:1	17:244	736
37:3	14:22	128–129
37:5	15:398; 17:54	473, 658
37:6[o]	14:58 [37:7]	151
37:7	17:244	736
37:8	17:244[c]	736[c]
37:12	17:248	738
37:14	17:248[x]	738[x]
37:15	17:248[x]	738[x]
37:16	17:226	729
37:18	17:226[c]	729[c]

37:19	17:226	729
37:21	17:336	775
37:26	17:336	775
38:4[o]	15:378 [38:5]	466 [38:5]
39:13[o]	15:220 [39:14]	401 [39:14]
40:6[o,13]	15:280, 292	428, 434
40:7	15:280 [40:8], 292 [40:8]	428 [40:8][14], 434 [40:8]
40:8	15:316; 17:44 [40:9]	443, 654 [40:9]
40:9	15:316[c]	443[c]
40:17[o]	17:226 [40:18]	729[40:18]
41:1[o]	17:378 [41:2]	791 [41:2]
41:6[o]	17:268 [41:7]	748 [41:7]
41:8[o]	15:390 [41:9]	470 [41:9]
41:10	17:288	755
41:11	17:288[c]	755[c]
42:2[o]	14:54 [42:3]	149 [42:3]
44:2[o]	17:408 [44:3]	803 [44:3]
45[o]	14:258	241
45:7[o]	14:244[c] [45:8]	235[c] [45:8]
45:9	15:140 [45:10]	364 [45:10]
45:14[o]	15:140 [45:15, 16]	364 [45:15, 16]
46:1[o]	17:248 [46:1]	738 [46:1]
46:2	17:248 [46:2]	738 [46:2]
49:8[o]	15:236 [49:9]	407 [49:9]
49:12[o]	15:236 [49:13]	407 [49:13]
49:14[o]	15:236 [49:15]; 348 [49:15]	407 [49:15], 619 [49:15]
49:15	15:236 (twice) [49:16]; 16:348[q] [49:16]	407 (twice) [49:16], 619[q] [49:16]
49:20[o]	17:362 [49:21]	785 [49:21]
50:15	17:80	669
50:16	17:398	799
50:17	17:398[c]	799[c]
51:3[o]	15:378–380 [51:5]	466–467 [51:5]
51:4[o]	15:378–380 [51:6]	466–467 [51:6]
51:5	15:44 [51:7], 194 [51:7]	320, 389 [51:7]
51:10[o]	15:366 [51:12], 370 [51:12]	461 [51:12], 462 [51:12]
51:11[o]	14:360–362 [51:13]	283 [51:13]
51:12	14:360–362 [51:14]	283[51:14]
51:17[o]	15:380 [51:19]; 17:64 [51:19]	467 [51:19], 662 [51:19]
51:18[o]	17:96 [51:20]	674 [51:20]
52:1[o]	17:238 [52:3], 268 [52:3]	734 [52:3], 748 [52:3]
52:2[o]	17:314 [52:4]	766 [52:4]
53:1	17:50[c]	656[c]
54:5[o]	17:288 [54:7]	755 [54:7]
55:3[o]	17:208[q]	722[q]

55:5	17:208	722
55:6	17:208[c]	722[c]
55:7[o]	17:208[c]	722[c]
55:12[o]	17:276 [55:13]	751 [55:13]
55:13	17:276–278[x]	751[x]
55:17[o]	17:94 [55:18]	674 [55:18]
55:23[o]	15:92 [55:24]	340 [55:24]
56:11[o]	17:248 [56:12]	738 [56:12]
58:3[o]	15:194 [58:4]; 17:362 [58:4]	389 [58:4], 785 [58:4]
58:4	17:328 [58:5]	772 [58:5]
58:5	17:328 [58:6]	772 [58:6]
58:10[o]	17:204 [58:11]	721 [58:11]
59:7[o]	17:314 [59:8]	766 [59:8]
60:1	17:408	803
60:2	17:408[c]	803[c]
60:4[o]	17:402 [60:6]	801
60:8[o]	17:408 [60:10]	802 [60:10]
61	17:54	658
62	17:54	658
62:12	16:44	493
64:3	17:314	766
66:10	15:88	338
66:18	17:84	671
68:5[o]	17:376 [68:6]	790–791 [68:6]
68:10[o]	17:226 [68:11]	729 [68:11]
68:17[o]	14:274–276 [68:18]; 15:104 [68:18]	250 [68:18], 347 [68:18]
68:18	14:274–276 [68:19], 328 [68:19]; 15:298 [68:19]	250 [68:19], 269 [68:19], 436 [68:19]
68:19	14:274–276[c] [68:20]	250[c] [68:20]
69:7[o]	17:252 [69:8]	739 [69:8]
69:8	17:152 [69:9]	697 [69:9]
69:9	17:152 [69:10]	697 [69:10]
69:28[o]	14:94 [69:29]	170
71:20	15:390	470
71:21	15:390[c]	470[c]
72:1	17:96	675
72:2	17:386	794
72:18	15:94	341
73:2	15:90	339
73:6	17:62	661
73:12	15:60	328
73:17	15:60[q], 90	328[q], 339
73:25	17:146	694
73:26	17:54[c]	658[c]
74:2	17:96	674

75:2°	17:386 [75:3]	794 [75:3]
75:6°	17:388 [75:7]	795 [75:7]
75:7	17:362 [75:8]	786 [75:8]
77:13°	15:60 [77:14]	328 [77:14]
78:8	15:210; 16:282	396, 591
78:11	16:224	565
78:18	17:148	695
78:19	17:148	695
78:22	15:398	473
78:30	17:102[c]	677[c]
78:32	16:224	565
78:41	17:148	695
78:50	15:230	404
80:1°	15:58 [80:2]	327 [80:2]
80:3°	15:58 [80:4]	327 [80:4]
81:11	15:76 [81:12]; 17:36	334 [81:12], 651
81:12	15:76 [81:13]; 17:36	334 [81:13], 651
81:13	17:36[c], 68 [81:14]	651[c], 664 [81:14]
81:14	17:68[c] [81:15]	664[c] [81:15]
82:1	14:244[c]	234[c]
82:3	17:386	794
82:6	14:194, 244; 16:100[15]	213, 234, 516[16]
84:12	17:54[c]	658[c]
86:4	17:80	669
86:5	17:80	669
86:10[17]	14:52	148
86:15	14:56[c]	150[c]
88:10[o,18]	15:220	401
88:11[19]	15:220	401
88:12[20]	15:220	401
88:13	17:94 [88:14]	674 [88:14]
89:35°	15:258 [89:36, 37]	418 [89:36, 37]
89:36	15:258 [89:36, 37]	418 [89:36, 37]
89:48°	15:230 [89:49]	405 [89:49]
90:2	14:42	143
90:3	15:388	469
90:10	15:90	339
91:11	15:100	346
92:1°	17:94 [92:2]	674 [92:2]
92:2	17:94 [92:3]	674 [92:3]
92:7°	15:60 [92:8]	328 [92:8]
92:11°	17:288 [92:12]	755 [92:12]
93:1	15:58	328
94:1	17:288	755
94:2	17:288	755

94:7	17:62, 148	661, 695
94:12	15:386	469
94:17	15:230	405
94:20	17:390	796
94:23	15:72	332
95:6	17:90	672
95:7	14:150; 17:148[c]	193, 695[c]
95:8	14:150[x]; 15:84; 17:148	193[x], 337, 695
95:9	14:150[c]; 17:148	193[c], 695–696
95:10	14:166	200
95:11	14:166; 17:120 [9:5, 11]	200, 684
97:7	14:244; 15:34	234, 315
97:9	14:244	234
99:6	16:264	583
101:4	17:388	795
101:6	17:366, 388[x]	787, 795[x]
101:7	17:304	762
102:12[o]	14:42 [102:13]	143
102:13	17:96 [102:14]	674 [102:14]
102:24[o]	14:42 [102:25]	143
102:26	14:46; 16:368 [102:27]	144, 628 [102:27]
102:27	14:42 [102:28], 46 (twice)[21]	143 [102:28], 144 (twice)[22]
103:2	17:58	659–660
103:8	14:56[c]	150[c]
103:11	14:56	150
103:17	14:56–58	150
103:19	15:58	328
103:20	15:34, 100	314–315, 345
104	14:60; 15:36	152, 316
104:1	14:60	151
104:4	15:34	314
104:15	17:234	732
104:21	15:62	329
104:29	15:38, 58, 236	317, 327, 407
104:30	14:360; 15:38, 236	282, 317, 407
105:14	17:394	797
105:15	16:244	572
105:25	15:70	331
106:19	17:136	691
106:20	17:136	691
106:31	16:38	490
106:37	15:96	343
109:2	17:314	766
109:6	17:98	675
109:28	17:104	677

110:1	14:204, 246[23]; 15:296, 300, 314	217, 236[24], 435, 437, 442
110:2	15:300	437
110:3	17:44	654
110:4	15:284, 290; 17:120	431, 433, 684
110:5	14:248[25]; 16:360	236[26], 624
110:6	16:360	624
111:10	17:28	648
112:5	17:336, 344	775, 779
112:7	17:54, 248, 250[c]	658, 738, 739[c]
112:8	17:248[c]	738[c]
112:9	17:378[c]	791[c]
113:7	17:362	786
115:1	17:64	662
115:3	14:46	145
115:5	17:142	693
115:8	17:142[x]	693[x]
115:9	17:54	658
115:17	15:220	401
116:6	17:316	767
116:12	17:58	660
118:6	17:248[c]	738[c]
118:8	17:56[c]	658[c]
118:9	17:56[c]	658[c]
119:9	17:360	785
119:18	16:258	579
119:22	17:238	734
119:36	17:228	730
119:39	17:238	734
119:42	17:324	770
119:44	17:46	654
119:45	16:52–54; 17:46	496, 654
119:46	17:162	701
119:51	17:46	654
119:55	17:94	674
119:61	17:46	654
119:62	17:94	674
119:63	17:276	750
119:66	17:26	647
119:68	14:58	150
119:69	17:312	766
119:71	15:386	469
119:95	17:46	654
119:98	17:26	647
119:99	17:26	647
119:100	17:26	647

119:105	16:258	579
119:106	15:214; 17:110	398, 680
119:110	17:46	654
119:112	17:46	654
119:116	17:56	659
119:130	16:258	579
119:136	17:206	721
119:137	14:58	151
119:139	17:152	697
119:147	17:94	674
119:148	17:94	674
119:157	17:46	654–655
119:164	17:94	674
120:2	17:314, 318	766, 768
120:5	17:278	751
120:6	17:278–280	751–752
122:6	17:96	674
123	17:54	658
125:1	16:78	506
125:2	16:78[c]	506[c]
125:3	15:388	469
126:2	17:204	721
126:5	15:390	470
127:1	17:366, 408	787, 803
127:2	17:366[c]	787[c]
130:3	16:14	481
130:4	15:380; 17:60	467, 660
130:6	17:54[c]	658[c]
131:1	17:236	733
133:1	17:270, 364 [133:2]	748, 786 [133:2]
135:6	14:46[c]; 15:14	145[c], 305
137	17:268	748
137:7	16:312; 17:264	604, 745
137:8	16:312; 17:288	604, 755
137:9	16:312[c]	604[c]
139:2	14:54	149
139:4	14:54	149
139:7	14:360	282
139:8	14:46	144
139:9	14:46[c]	144[c]
139:21	17:258	743
139:22	17:258[c]	743[c]
140:3[o]	17:314 [140:4]	766 [140:4]
140:10[o]	17:98 [140:11]	675 [140:11]
141:3	17:210	723

141:4	17:278	751
141:5	17:326	771
143:2	15:192	388
143:10	14:362; 16:14	283, 481
144:1	17:408	803
144:2	17:408[c]	803[c]
145:3	14:60	152
145:13	14:42–44	143
145:18	17:98	676
146:2	15:220	401
146:3	17:56	658
146:4	15:228	404
146:9	17:376	791
147:5	14:54	149
147:6	17:284	754
147:9	15:62	329
147:10	17:56, 408	658, 803
147:13	17:408	803
147:19	15:350; 16:104	456, 517
147:20	15:350; 16:104	456, 517
148:2	15:100	345
148:5	15:6, 36	301, 316
148:6	16:368[c]	627[c]
148:8	15:94	341
148:12	17:360	785
149:5	17:90	672
149:6	17:410	803

Proverbs

1:7	17:28[c]	648[c]
1:8	17:356	784
1:11	17:24	646
1:19	17:228	730
1:20	17:30	648
1:23	15:386	469
1:24	15:346; 17:86	454, 671
1:28	17:86[x]	671[x]
2:4	17:28	648
2:16	17:218	727
3:7	17:32	649
3:11	15:386	469
3:12	15:386	469
3:13	17:30	648

3:24	17:248	738
3:25	17:248[c]	738[c]
3:27	17:344	779
3:28	17:344	779
3:29	17:318	768
3:31	17:244, 316	736, 767
3:33	17:366 (twice)	787 (twice)
3:34	17:64	662
3:35	17:362	785
4:5	17:30	648
4:14	17:24	646
4:23	17:38	652
4:24	17:322	769
5:3	17:218	727
5:18	17:350	781–782
5:19	17:350[c]	781[c]
5:20	17:350	782
5:21	17:350[c]	782[c]
6:1	17:264	745
6:2	17:264	745
6:6	17:232	732
6:16	17:246, 286, 304	736, 755, 762
6:17	17:246, 286, 304	736, 755, 762
6:20	17:356	784
6:21	17:356[c]	784[c]
6:23	17:326	771
6:24[1]	17:218 (twice)	727 (twice)
6:25	17:204	720
6:30	17:330	773
6:32	17:218[c]	727[c]
6:34	17:292	756
7:11	17:352	782
7:25	17:218	727
8:[o]	15:12	304
8:1	17:30[c]	648[c]
8:6	17:30	648
8:15	17:388	795
8:16	17:388[c]	795[c]
8:22	15:10–12	303–304
8:23	15:10–12	303–304
8:26	15:36	316
8:36	17:200	719
9:7	17:328	772
9:8	17:328	772
9:13	17:352	782

9:16	17:32	649
9:18	17:218	727
10:1	17:358	784
10:3	17:226	729
10:4	17:230, 232	731–732, 732
10:5	17:230	732
10:9	17:10	640
10:11	17:282	753
10:12	17:310	765
10:14	17:320	769
10:17	17:326	771
10:18	17:314	766
10:19	17:320 (twice)	768–769, 769
10:22	17:222	728–729
10:23	17:204	721
10:24	15:58; 17:250	328, 739
10:25	17:10	640
10:26	17:370	788
10:27	15:92	340
10:28	17:56	659
10:29	17:10	640
11:1	17:334	775
11:2	17:236	733
11:3	17:22	645
11:5	17:22	645
11:9	17:210	722
11:11	17:210, 412	722, 804
11:12	17:252	739
11:13	17:318, 320	768 (twice)
11:14	17:386	794
11:15	17:264	745
11:17	17:200	719
11:18	17:10	640
11:19	17:10[c]	640[c]
11:22	17:204	720
11:24	17:344	779
11:25	17:344[c]	779[c]
11:26	17:334	775
11:28	17:226	730
11:29	17:366	787
12:1°	17:326 [11:32]	771 [11:32]
12:3	15:58; 17:10 [12:2]	328, 640 [12:2]
12:9	17:236 [12:8]	733 [12:8]
12:10°	17:268 (twice) [12:9]	747 [12:9], 748 [12:9]
12:11	17:230	732

12:14[o]	17:210 [12:13]	722 [12:13]
12:15	17:276	750
12:16[o]	17:208 [12:15]	722 [12:15]
12:17	17:296	759
12:22[o]	17:296 [12:21]	759 [12:21]
12:28	16:20	483
13:1	17:328	772
13:2	17:210	722
13:3	17:320	769
13:4	17:232	732
13:5	17:296	759
13:9	15:60	328
13:15	17:22	645
13:18	17:70, 326	664, 771
13:20	17:276, 278	750, 751
13:21	17:10	640
13:24	17:354	783
13:25	15:40	318
14:1	17:350, 352	782 (twice)
14:3	17:322	769
14:6	17:32	649
14:7	17:278	751
14:9	17:278	751
14:11	17:366 (twice)	787 (twice)
14:12	17:32	649
14:14	17:278	751
14:15	17:318	768
14:16	17:250	739
14:17	17:208	722
14:21	17:378–380	791
14:23	17:230	732
14:24	17:234	733
14:26	17:54	658
14:29	17:286	755
14:30	17:268	747
14:31	17:332	774
14:32	16:20	483
14:34	17:412	804
15:2	17:210	722
15:3	14:46; 15:62	144, 329
15:4	17:210[c]	722[c]
15:5	17:326	771
15:6	17:366, 366–368	787 (twice)
15:7	17:210[c]	722[c]
15:8	17:76, 398[c]	667, 799[c]

15:10	17:326	771
15:11	14:54	149
15:18	17:286	755
15:21	17:204–206	721
15:23	17:210	722
15:24	17:10	640–641
15:25	17:246, 368	736–737, 787
15:27	17:228	730
15:28	17:210	722–723
15:32	17:326	771
15:33	17:236	733
16:1	17:210	723
16:2	14:54	149
16:3	17:54	658
16:4	14:94; 15:14, 66	170, 305, 330
16:5	17:64, 246	662, 737
16:8	17:198	718
16:9	15:64, 74, 78	330, 332, 335
16:11	17:334	775
16:12	17:386	794
16:17	17:10	641
16:18	17:246	737
16:19	17:236	733
16:22	17:320	768
16:23	17:210	723
16:26	17:322	769
16:27	17:210[c]	723[c]
16:31	17:360	785
16:32	17:208, 286	722, 755
16:33	15:64; 17:132	329, 690
17:2	17:370	788
17:3	14:54	149–150
17:5	17:206, 226	721, 729
17:9	17:310	765
17:10	17:326	771
17:13	17:346	780
17:14	17:280	752
17:15	17:316	767
17:17	17:274	750
17:18	17:264	745
17:19	17:280	752
17:20	17:318	768
17:22	17:206	721
17:23	17:390	796
17:24	17:320 (twice)	768 (twice)

17:27	17:252	739
17:28	17:320	769
18:6	17:322	769
18:7	17:320	769
18:8	17:312	766
18:10	17:54[c]	658[c]
18:12	17:236[c], 246	733[c], 737
18:13	17:210	723
18:14	17:206[c]	721[c]
18:17	17:386	795
18:18	17:132	690
18:19	17:364	786
18:21	17:210	723
18:22	15:150	368
18:24	17:274	750
19:1	17:226	729
19:3	14:174	202
19:4	17:278[c]	751[c]
19:5	17:296, 310	759, 765
19:6	17:278	751
19:7	17:278[c]	751[c]
19:8	17:200	719
19:11	17:208, 252, 286	722, 739, 755
19:13	17:352	782–783
19:14	15:150; 17:350	368, 782
19:17	17:336, 380	775, 791
19:18	17:354	783
19:21	14:74[c]	161[c]
19:23	17:60	660
19:24	17:232	732
19:26	17:358	784
19:28	17:210	723
20:1	17:214	725
20:3	17:280	752
20:4	17:232	732
20:6	17:238, 296	734, 759
20:7	17:10	641
20:8	17:386	795
20:9	15:192; 16:14	388, 481
20:10	17:334–336	775
20:11	17:362	785
20:13	17:216	726
20:14	17:336	775
20:16	17:264	745
20:18	17:406[c]	802[c]

20:19	17:312, 318	766, 768
20:20	17:358	784
20:21	17:228	730
20:22	17:288	755
20:23	17:336[c]	775[c]
20:24	15:58, 64	328, 330
20:25	17:116	682
21:1	15:58, 64	328, 330
21:2	17:32	649
21:3	17:194	716
21:4	17:246	737
21:5	17:232	732
21:6	17:332	774
21:7	17:390	796
21:9	17:352	783
21:13	17:380, 408	792, 803
21:14	17:378	791
21:15	17:44	654
21:17	17:214, 234	725, 733
21:19	17:352	783
21:20	17:344	779
21:22	17:406	802
21:23	17:210	723
21:25	17:232	732
21:26	17:232[c], 344	732[c], 779
21:27	17:76[c], 398	667[c], 799
22:1	17:238	734
22:5	17:22	645
22:6	17:354	783
22:9	17:380	791
22:13	17:232	732
22:14	17:218	727
22:15	17:354	783
22:22	17:332	774
22:23	17:332[c]	774[c]
22:24	17:208	722
22:25	17:208[c]	722[c]
22:26	17:264	745
22:27	17:264[c]	745[c]
22:28	17:330	773
22:29	17:232	732
23:3	17:214	725
23:6	17:344	779
23:7	17:344[c]	779[c]
23:8	17:344[c]	779[c]

23:9	17:30	648
23:10	17:330[c], 376	773[c], 791
23:11	17:376	791
23:13	17:354	783
23:14	17:354	783
23:17	17:12, 316	641, 767
23:20	17:214	725
23:21	17:214[c]	725[c]
23:22	17:356, 358	784 (twice)
23:24	17:356[c]	784[c]
23:25	17:356[c]	784[c]
23:26	17:218[c]	727[c]
23:27	17:218[c]	727[c]
23:29	17:214	725
23:30	17:214	725
23:31	17:214[c]	725[c]
23:32	17:214[c]	725[c]
24:1	17:12, 278	641, 751
24:2	17:278[c]	751[c]
24:3	17:366	787
24:4	17:366[c]	787[c]
24:5	17:248	738
24:6	17:248[c], 406[c]	738[c], 802[c]
24:8	15:198	391
24:10	17:252	740
24:11	17:282	753
24:12	17:282	753
24:16	16:14, 96	481, 513
24:17	17:268	748
24:21	17:398	799
24:22	17:398[c]	799[c]
24:23	17:386	795
24:24	17:316	767
24:25	17:326	771
24:26	17:322	770
24:29	17:288	755
24:30	17:232	732
25:5	17:392 [25:4]	796 [25:4]
25:8	17:314	766–767
25:9	17:314[c], 318	766[c], 768
25:10	17:314[c]	766[c]
25:11	17:322	770
25:12	17:326–328	771
25:13	17:370	788
25:14	17:238	734

25:17	17:264	746
25:18	17:310	765
25:21	17:256	742
25:22	17:256	742
25:24	17:352[c]	783[c]
25:25	15:40	318
25:26	17:250	739
25:27	17:244	736
25:28	17:202	720
26:1	17:362	786
26:2	17:104	677
26:4	17:328	772
26:5	17:324	770
26:6	17:370	788
26:8	17:364	786
26:12	17:32	649
26:14	17:232	732
26:16	17:238	734
26:17	17:258	743
26:19	17:206	721
26:20	17:312	766
26:22	17:312[c]	766[c]
26:24	17:280[c], 318	752[c], 768
26:25[o]	17:318[x]	768[x]
26:26	17:280[x]	752[x]
26:28	17:316, 318	767, 768
27:1	17:54	658
27:2	17:240	735
27:3	17:208	722
27:6	17:316, 328	767, 771
27:7	15:40	318
27:9	17:276	750
27:10	17:274	750
27:13	17:264[c]	745[c]
27:14	17:316	767
27:15	17:352[c]	783[c]
27:18	17:370	788
27:22	17:322	769
27:23	17:366	787
28:1	17:248, 250	738, 739
28:2	17:412	804
28:4	17:258	743
28:5	17:24, 26–28	646, 647
28:6	17:226	729–730
28:7	17:278	751

28:8	17:342	777–778[2]
28:9	17:70	664
28:11	17:226	730
28:13	15:382	467
28:15	17:390	796
28:16	17:390[c]	796[c]
28:17	17:286	755
28:19	17:232	732
28:23	17:328	771
28:24	17:330, 358	773, 784
28:26	17:32	649
28:27	17:380 (twice)	791, 792
29:1	17:328	771
29:4	17:386 (twice), 390	794–795, 795, 796
29:5	17:316	767
29:9	17:328	772
29:11	17:36	651
29:12	17:390	796
29:15	17:354	783
29:17	17:354[c]	783[c]
29:19	17:368	787
29:20	17:210, 320	723, 769
29:21	17:366	787
29:22	17:208	722
29:23	17:236, 246	733, 737
29:24	17:200, 330	719, 773
29:25	17:250	739
29:26	17:56, 398	658, 799
29:27	17:258	743
30:5	17:28, 54[c]	647–648, 658[c]
30:6	16:280; 17:28, 72	591, 647–648, 665
30:8	17:114, 222	681, 729
30:14	17:332	774
30:17	17:358	784
30:20	17:218	727
30:21	15:164; 17:244	374, 736
30:22	17:244[x], 370	736[x], 788
30:23	15:164; 17:244[x], 370[c]	374–375, 736[x], 788[c]
31:1[3]	17:386	795
31:6	17:234	732
31:11	17:350	782
31:22	17:234	733
31:25	17:234[c]	733[c]

Ecclesiastes

1:4	16:368[c]	627[c]
1:16	17:236	734
1:17	17:34	650
2:2[o]	17:206 [2:3]	721 [2:3]
2:26[o]	17:228 [2:27]	730 [2:27]
3:1	17:36	651
3:11	17:36	651
3:12	17:222	729
3:13	17:222–224	729
3:18	15:228	404
3:19	15:38, 228	317, 404
3:20	15:228, 236 [3:12]	404, 407
3:21	15:228	404
4:5	17:232 [4:1]	732 [4:1]
4:6[o]	17:232 [4:2]	732 [4:2]
4:8[o]	17:228 [4:4]	730 [4:4]
4:9	17:274 [4:5]	750 [4:5]
4:13[o]	17:390 [4:9]	796 [4:9]
5:1	17:68–70	664
5:2	17:90	672
5:4	17:116	682
5:5	17:116	682
5:8	17:332	774
5:10	17:228	730
5:18	17:224	729
5:19	17:224[x]	729[x]
5:20	17:224[x]	729[x]
6:1	17:224	729
6:2	17:224, 230	729, 731
6:11	17:226	730
7:1	17:238–240	734
7:2	17:206	721
7:3	17:206[c]	721[c]
7:4	17:206[c]	721[c]
7:5	17:328	771
7:7	17:68, 332	663, 774
7:9	17:208	722
7:10	16:282	592
7:14	17:46	655
7:15	15:60	328
7:18	15:60	328
7:20	15:192	388
7:21	17:252	739–740

7:26	17:352	783
7:29	14:94–96; 15:52, 182; 17:34	171, 324, 384, 650
8:1	17:320 [7:30]	768 [7:30]
8:2[o]	17:398 [8:1]	799 [8:1]
8:11	17:62 [8:10]	661 [8:10]
8:12[o]	15:60–62 [8:11]	328 [8:11]
8:14[o]	15:60 [8:13]	328 [8:13]
9:2[o]	15:60 [9:4]	328 [9:4]
9:8[o]	17:234 [9:10]	733 [9:10]
9:9	15:164 [9:12]; 17:224	375 [9:12], 729
9:10	17:224[c]	729[c]
9:11	15:64	329
9:15	17:346	780
9:18[o]	17:30 [9:20]	648 [9:20]
10:2	17:320 [9:22]	768 [9:22]
10:4[o]	17:310 [10:1]	765 [10:1]
10:5[o]	17:362 [10:2], 390 [10:2]	786 [10:2], 796 [10:2]
10:6[o]	17:362 [10:3], 390 [10:3]	786 [10:3], 796 [10:3]
10:16[o]	17:390 [10:13]	796 [10:13]
10:17[o]	17:390[c] [10:14]	796[c] [10:14]
10:20	17:314	766
11:1	17:344	779
11:9	17:360	785
11:10	17:360[c]	785[c]
12:1	17:360	785
12:2	17:360[c]	785[c]
12:3	17:360[c]	785[c]
12:7	15:48, 236 [12:9]	323, 407 [12:9]
12:12[o]	17:34 [12:14]	650 [12:14]
12:13[o]	17:28 [12:15]	648 [12:15]
12:14	16:354–356 [12:16]	622 [12:16]

Song of Solomon

6:8	15:140, 142	364, 365
6:9	15:142	365
6:10	15:142	365
8:6	17:292	756

Isaiah

1:2	17:60	660
1:3	17:30	649
1:10	17:324	771
1:11	17:76	667

1:16	15:360, 382; 17:84	459, 468, 671
1:17	15:382; 17:84[c]	468[1], 671[c]
1:18	16:30; 17:84	487, 671
1:23	17:324, 390	771, 796
1:25	15:386	469
2:2	15:282; 16:122	429, 525
2:8	17:136	691
3	17:412	804
3:1[2]	17:56	659
3:2[o]	17:56[c]	659[c]
3:4[o]	17:390 [3:5]	796 [3:5]
3:5	17:362 [3:6]	785 [3:6]
3:7[o]	17:412 [3:8]	804 [3:8]
3:9[o]	17:238 [3:10]	734 [3:10]
3:12[o]	17:390 [3:13]	796 [3:13]
3:14[o]	17:332 [3:15], 390–392 [3:15]	774 [3:15], 796 [3:15]
3:15	17:332[c] [3:16]	774[c] [3:16]
3:16	17:220	728
4:3	14:92	170
5:4	14:148, 172[c]	193, 201[c]
5:7	17:332[c]	774[c]
5:8	17:332	774
5:11	17:214	725
5:12	17:214	725
5:13	17:30	649
5:16	14:58	151
5:19	17:62	661
5:20	17:316	767
5:21	17:32	649
5:22	17:214	725
5:23	17:392	796
5:26	17:408	803
6	14:60; 15:104	152, 347
6:1	14:30, 250	133, 237
6:2	14:56; 15:36 (twice)	150, 315 (twice)[3]
6:3	14:56; 15:100	150, 345
6:8	14:382	290
6:9	14:382; 15:70	290, 332
6:10	14:172; 15:82	201, 336
7:12	17:54	658
7:14	15:280	428
8:11	14:294	257
8:12	17:206[c]	721[c]
8:13	14:294 (twice); 17:206[c]	257 (twice), 721[c]
8:14	14:294, 296; 15:70	257 (twice), 331

8:19	17:150	696
8:20	16:250, 256	575, 578
9:6	14:304; 15:288, 300	260, 432, 436
9:7	15:300; 16:360	436, 624
9:15	17:416	805
10:12	17:392	796
10:20	15:398	473
11:1	15:258, 260[c], 280	418, 419[c], 428
11:2	14:362; 15:260	283, 419
11:4	15:14	305
11:11	16:342	617
11:12	16:342[c]	617[c]
13:9	16:346[c]	619[c]
13:10	16:346[c]	619[c]
14:1	14:112; 16:342	179, 617
17:8	17:136	691
19:11	17:34	650
19:14	15:70	331
19:18	16:122	525
19:22	15:380	467
22:8	17:56 [22:7]	659 [22:7]
22:12	17:206	721
22:13	17:206[x]	721[x]
22:15	17:392	796
22:16	17:392[c]	796[c]
23:9	17:362	786
24	17:412	804
25:6	16:122	525
26:10	14:148; 15:200	193, 392
26:19	16:348	619
27:12[o]	16:342 [27:14]	617 [27:14]
27:13[o,4]	16:342	617
28:1	17:214	725
28:3	17:214[c]	725[c]
28:7	17:214[c]	725[c]
28:8	17:214[c]	725[c]
28:12	14:168	200
28:13	14:168; 15:82, 350	200, 336, 456
28:15	17:62	661
28:16	17:66	663
28:29	14:38[c]	138[c]
29:8	15:40	318
29:10	14:168; 15:70	200, 331
29:13	14:168; 16:282; 17:74, 76	200, 591, 667 (twice)
29:14	14:168; 16:282[c]; 17:34	200, 591[c], 650

29:15	17:62	661
30:2	17:56 [30:1], 404[c]	658–659 [30:1], 801[c]
30:8	16:250	575
30:9	17:420	807
30:10	17:420[c]	807[c]
30:33	16:370, 372	629 (twice)
31:1	17:56	659
31:3	14:40	140
31:6	17:406	802
31:8[o]	17:406[x]	802[x]
32:5	17:316	767
32:8	17:316[c], 362–364	767[c], 786
33:11	17:34	650
33:14	17:10	641
33:15[o]	17:10[x]	641[x]
34:4	16:368	628
35:4	14:324	268 [25:4]
35:5	14:324	268 [25:5]
35:6	14:324	268 [25:6]
38:3	17:22	645
38:17	15:230; 17:22	405, 645
38:18	15:222	402
38:19	15:222	402
40:2	15:388	470
40:3	14:300	259
40:18	17:138	692
40:25	14:56	150
40:28	14:54, 60	150, 152
40:31	17:56–58 [40:29]	659 [40:29]
41:10	17:248	738
41:13	17:250[c]	739[c]
41:14	17:250	739
41:20	14:56	150
42:1	14:88, 340, 348, 362, 364; 15:284	166–167, 274, 277, 283, 284, 430
42:3	15:396	472
42:4	16:122	525
42:8	14:340	274
42:14	14:44	143
43:10	14:44	143
43:28	17:156	699
44:5	17:138[c]	692[c]
44:6	14:44, 48 [44:1]	143, 147 [44:1]
44:8[o]	14:48 [44:3]	147
44:10[o]	17:138[x]	692[x]
44:18[o]	17:142 [44:12, 13]	693 [44:12, 13]

44:24	15:4, 48	300, 323
44:25°	17:150 [44:20]	696 [44:20]
45:4	14:98	172
45:5	14:48	147
45:6	15:4	300
45:7	15:4, 16 [43:7], 66 (twice)	300, 306, 330 (twice)
45:12	15:12, 94	304, 341
45:21	14:48–50	147
45:22	14:50; 16:122; 17:124[c]	147, 525, 686[c]
45:23	15:12; 16:122[c]; 17:124[c]	304, 525[c], 686[c]
46:5	17:138	692
46:6	17:138, 146	692, 695
46:7	17:146	695
46:9	14:50	147
46:10	14:74[c]	161[c]
47:13	17:150	696
47:14	17:150	696
48:1	17:78	668
48:8	15:194	389
48:10	15:386	469
48:16	14:360	282
48:18	17:412	804
49:4	16:236–238	569
49:6	15:304	439
49:7	15:304	439
49:23	17:392	797
50:1	14:142	190
50:6	15:304	439
50:7	17:252	740
50:8	17:252[c]	740[c]
51:4	14:18	127
51:6	16:348, 368	619, 628
51:7	17:156, 248	699, 738
51:12	17:248	738
51:16	14:322	267
52:5	17:166[c]	703[c]
53:1	15:254	417
53:2	15:304	439
53:3	15:304	439
53:6	15:308	440
53:10	15:256, 292	417, 434
53:11°	15:330[5]; 16:26	449[6], 486
53:12	15:292, 294	433, 434
54:13	16:6	478
54:16	15:16, 66	306, 330

55:1	15:346	454
55:4	16:122	525
55:5	15:288; 16:122[c]	432, 525[c]
55:6	17:86	671
55:7	15:380	467
55:9	15:60	328
56:2	17:176[c]	708[c]
56:3	16:122	525
56:4	17:176[c]	708[c]
56:5	16:50	495
56:6	17:176[c]	708[c]
56:10[o]	17:416 [57:2]	805 [57:2]
57:1[o]	15:222 [57:5]	402 [57:5]
57:2	15:222 [57:6]	402 [57:6]
57:5	17:136 [57:9]	691 [57:9]
57:9	17:412 [57:13]	804 [57:13]
57:10[o]	17:412[c] [57:14]	804[c] [57:14]
57:13	17:412[c] [57:17]	804[c] [57:17]
57:15[o]	15:28 [57:19]	311
57:16[o]	15:48 [57:20], 388 [57:20]	323 [57:20], 469–470 [57:20]
57:17	17:228 [57:21]	730 [57:21]
57:19	15:360	459
58:1	17:414	805
58:5	17:104 [58:56]	677
58:6	17:104 [58:56], 380[c]	677–678, 791
58:7	17:376, 380	791, 791–792
58:8[o]	17:380[q]	791–792[q]
59:1	17:54, 98 [59:12]	658, 676 [59:12]
59:2	17:98–100 [59:12]	676 [59:12]
59:4	17:22, 164	645, 702
59:5[o]	17:22[q]	645[q]
59:15	17:34	650
59:21	16:116, 272–274	523, 587
61:1	14:364; 15:284, 288; 17:284	284, 430, 432, 754
61:6	16:244	572
61:7	15:388–390	470
61:8	17:198	718
63:5	14:340	274
63:9	14:288; 15:100	254, 346
63:10	14:360	282
63:11	14:360	282
63:15	15:28	311
63:16	17:146	694
64:6[o]	15:384 [64:10]	468 [64:10]
65:1	15:346	454

65:6	14:94	170
65:8	17:276	750
65:9	14:112	179
65:10	14:112	179
65:16	17:120, 124[c]	684, 686[c]
65:17	16:378	632
65:20	17:360	785
65:24	17:100	676
66:2	15:380–382; 17:64	467, 662
66:3	17:78	668
66:15	16:346	619
66:16	16:346[c]	619[c]
66:21	16:122	525
66:22	16:378–380	632
66:24	16:370[c]	629[c]

Jeremiah

1:5	15:374–376	464
1:6	17:236	733
1:7	17:236[c], 412	733[c], 805
1:8	17:412[c]	805[c]
1:17	17:414	805
1:18	17:414[c]	805[c]
1:19	17:414[c]	805[c]
2:8	17:416	806
2:11	17:138	692
2:34	17:332	774
2:35	17:48	655
3:12	15:382 [3:7]; 16:342 [3:7]	467 [3:7], 617 [3:7]
3:13	15:380 [3:8]	467 [3:8]
3:17[o]	16:124 [3:12]	525 [3:12]
3:18[o]	16:342 [3:13]	617 [3:13]
4:1	15:360	459
4:4	15:382; 16:166	467, 543
5	17:412	804
5:3	15:82	336
5:4	17:30	649
5:7	17:290	756
5:8	17:290[c]	756[c]
5:14	17:416	806
5:31	17:416	806
6:8	15:358	458
6:10	15:206	395

6:13	17:416	806
6:14	17:416[c]	806[c]
6:16	16:282–284; 17:70–72	592, 664
6:17	17:72	664
6:19	17:70	664
6:20	17:70	664
6:30	14:144	191
7:3	14:144	191
7:4	17:76, 194	667, 716
7:5	17:194	716
7:7	16:368[c]	627[c]
7:12	17:76	667
7:13	15:210	396 [8:13]
7:14	15:210; 17:76	396 [8:14], 667
7:15	15:210	396 [8:15]
7:16	15:210; 17:96	396 [8:15], 675
7:22	17:70	664
7:23	17:70	664
7:26[o]	17:72 [7:25]	664 [7:25]
7:31	17:136	691
8:2	17:262	745
8:7	17:30	649
8:9	17:416	806
9:3	17:314	766
9:5	17:304	762
10:2	17:150	696
10:8	17:142[c]	693[c]
10:10	14:40, 246[c]	140, 236[c]
10:14	17:142	693
10:15	17:142	693
10:21	17:416	806
10:23	15:64	330
10:24	15:386	469
11:13	17:136	691
11:20	17:288	755
12:1	15:62	328–329
12:16	17:120	684
13:18	17:324	771 [13:8]
14:11	17:96[c]	675[c]
14:12	17:96[c]	675[c]
14:13	17:416[c]	806[c]
14:14	17:416[c]	806[c]
14:15	17:416	806
14:18	17:416[c]	806[c]
15:10	17:414	805

15:11	17:414[c]	805[c]
15:15	17:288	755
16:4	17:262	745
16:7	17:270	748
17:5	17:56	659
17:7	15:398; 17:54	473, 658
17:9	15:194, 198	389, 391
17:10	14:54	150
17:11	17:198	718 [16:11]
17:21	17:170, 174[c]	705, 707[c]
17:22	17:170[c], 174[c]	705[c], 707[c]
18:6	14:144[c]	191[c]
18:8	15:360	459
18:9	14:66 [18:8–10]	155
18:10	14:66	155
18:18	17:78	668
18:19	17:98[c], 414	675[c], 805
18:21	17:98	675
18:22	17:98	675
20:7	17:414	805
20:12	17:288[c]	755[c]
20:14	17:102	677
20:15	17:68	663
21:4	17:408	803
21:12	17:386	795
22:3	17:386	795
22:4	17:386[c]	795[c]
22:13	17:332	774
22:21	17:72	664
22:24	14:112	179
23:5	15:300	436
23:6	14:326; 15:300	269, 436
23:9	17:152, 416	697, 806
23:10	17:152	697
23:11	17:152[c]	697[c]
23:16	17:420	807
23:21	16:234	568–569
23:23	14:54	150
23:24	14:46, 54–56	144, 150
25:3	15:186	386
25:4	15:186–188	386
25:5	16:368[c]	627[c]
25:8	16:124	525
25:9[o]	16:124[x]	525[x]
26:3	14:66	155

26:8	16:316	605
27:6	17:128	687
28	17:416	806
29:6	15:152	368
29:7	17:96	675
29:21	17:416[c]	806[c]
29:25	17:416	806
29:26	16:316; 17:416–418[x]	605, 806[x]
30:3	16:342	617
30:9	14:200; 15:258	215, 418
30:16	16:312	604
30:21	15:294	434
31:4	17:206	721
31:5	16:342	617
31:9	14:190	211
31:13[o]	17:206	721
31:15	15:222	402
31:18	15:210, 378	396, 466
31:31	14:382; 15:298; 16:112[c], 116, 124[c]	290, 436, 522[c], 523, 525–526[c]
31:32	15:298; 16:112[c], 116[c], 124[c]	436, 522[c], 523[c], 525–526[c]
31:33	16:6, 100, 112[c], 116, 124[c], 274[c]	478, 516, 522[c], 523, 525–526[c], 587[c]
31:34	15:394; 16:6, 118, 274[c]	471–472, 478, 523, 587[c]
31:36	15:94; 16:342	341, 617
32:18	14:46	145
32:19	15:56	327
32:29	17:136	691
32:37	16:78[c]	507[c]
32:39[1]	16:80	507
32:40	16:78	506–507
33:7	16:342	617
33:15	15:258	418
33:16	14:286, 326	253, 269
33:20	15:94; 16:78	341, 507
33:21	16:78	507
34	17:24, 368	646, 788
34:8	17:46	655
34:11[o]	17:46–48[x]	655[x]
34:12	14:282	252
34:15	17:48	655
34:16	17:48	655
35:2	17:70	664
35:5	17:356[c]	784[c]
35:6	17:356	784
36:23	17:72	664

37:10	17:408	803
38:17	14:66–68	156
43:2	17:420	807
44:16	17:72	664
44:17	16:284; 17:60	592, 660
45:3	17:68	663
48:10	17:258, 408	743, 802
50:6	17:418	806
50:15	17:288	755
50:20	16:30	487
50:29	16:312	604
50:30	16:312[c]	604[c]
50:34	16:312	604
51:11	16:312	604
51:16	15:62	329
51:24	16:312	604
51:34	16:312	604
51:49	16:312	604

Lamentations

1:21	17:288[c]	755[c]
1:22	17:288	755
2:14	17:418	806
3:22	14:58	150
3:27	15:386; 17:354	469, 783
3:28	15:386[c]; 17:354[c]	469[c], 783[c]
3:29	17:66	663
3:38	15:66	330
3:39	15:66–68	330
3:64	17:288 [3:59]	755 [3:59]
4:13	17:418	806
5:15	17:206	721

Ezekiel

1	14:60, 370	152, 285
1:6	15:34	315
1:27	17:138	692
1:28	17:138[c]	692[c]
2:4	15:350	456
2:5	15:350[c]	456[c]
2:6	17:414	805
2:7	15:352	456
2:17	15:352	456

2:21	15:352	456
3:8[o]	17:414 [2:18]	805
3:9[o]	17:414[c] [2:19]	805[c]
3:12	14:360; 15:352	282, 456
3:14	14:360	282
3:20	15:82	336
3:24	14:360	282
5:6	15:200	391
5:15	17:156	699
7	17:412	804
8:1	14:60[c]	152[c]
8:2	14:60[c]	152[c]
8:3	14:60[c]	152[c]
8:5	17:136	691
8:12	17:62	661
8:15	15:200	391
8:18	17:84	671
10:1	14:60[c]	152[c]
11:19	15:366, 370; 16:80	461, 462, 507
11:20	15:370; 16:80	462, 507
11:21	16:80	507
12:2	14:148; 15:328	193, 448
13:2[1]	17:418	806
13:5	17:410	803
14:9	15:70, 84	331, 337
14:10	15:84	337
14:11	15:84	337–338
14:14	17:102 [14:13]	676 [14:13]
16:25	17:244[c]	736[c]
16:26	17:404	801–802
16:36	17:244[c]	736[c]
16:49	17:214	725
17	17:406	802
18:4	15:186	386
18:6	17:290, 292	756, 757
18:7	17:342	778
18:8	17:342	778
18:20	15:230	405
18:21	15:358; 16:84	458, 509
18:25	14:144[c]; 16:84	191[c], 509
18:26	14:144[c]; 16:84 (twice)	191[c], 508–509, 509
18:27	14:144	191
18:28	15:358	458
18:31	14:144[c]; 16:12	192[c], 480
18:32	14:98, 144[c]	173, 192[c]

20:10	15:118	354
20:11	15:118	354
20:12	15:118, 374; 17:172	354, 464, 706
20:18	16:282	591
20:20	17:172[c]	706[c]
20:27[2]	17:160	700
20:28	17:160	700
20:30	17:84	671
20:31	17:84	671
20:41	16:342[c]	617[c]
20:42	16:342	617
21:21[o]	15:74 [21:26]	332 [21:26]
21:22[o]	15:74 [21:27]	332 [21:27]
21:25[o]	17:324 [21:30]	771 [21:30]
22:10	17:292	757
22:11	17:290, 292	756, 757
22:26	17:418	806
22:28	17:418	806
22:29	17:382	793
22:30	17:276	750
23:4	15:144	365
25:3	16:312–314	604
28:16	17:334	775
28:18	17:334[c]	775[c]
28:24	16:314	604
29:3	17:392	796
33:2[3]	17:414	805
33:11	14:98, 144, 150[c]	173, 192, 193[c]
33:12	16:84[c]	509[c]
33:13	16:84[c]	509[c]
33:14	14:144; 15:358	191–192, 458
33:15	14:144; 15:358	192, 458
33:16	15:358	458
33:30	17:78[c]	668[c]
33:31	17:78	668
33:32	17:78[c]	668[c]
34:2	17:418	806
34:23	15:288	432
35:5	16:314	604
36:20	17:166	703
36:26	15:370	462
36:27	16:10	479 [26:27]
36:31	15:380	467
36:32	15:380	467
37:9	15:238	408

37:14	14:360	282
37:21	16:342[c]	617[c]
37:22	16:342	617
37:25	15:296	435
43:2	14:60[c]	152[c]
43:3	14:60[c]	152[c]
43:10	15:380	467
44:8	17:416	805

Daniel

2:[o,1]	17:402	800
2:10	14:56[c]	150[c]
2:21	17:388	795
2:30	17:236	733
2:44	15:282, 296, 300	429, 435, 437
2:48	17:242	735
2:49	17:242[c]	735[c]
3:16	14:20; 17:248, 400	127, 738, 800
3:18	17:400	800
3:25	15:34	315
3:28	15:34	315
4:13	15:102	346
4:17	15:102; 17:388	346, 795
5:17	17:242	735
5:18	17:388	795
5:20	17:388 [5:19]	795 [5:19]
5:29	17:24[c], 242	646[c], 735
6	17:266	746
6:2[o]	17:242 [6:3]	735 [6:3]
6:7[o]	17:392 [6:8]	797 [6:8]
6:10[o]	17:90 [6:11], 94 [6:11], 400 [6:11]	673 [6:11], 674 [6:11], 800 [6:11]
7:9	14:60[c]	152[c]
7:10	14:60; 15:34, 100	151, 315, 345
7:13	16:358	624
7:14	15:296; 16:358, 366	435, 624, 627
7:22	16:338, 360	614, 624
7:27	16:360	624
8:13	15:106	348
8:16	15:36	315
9:3	17:106	678
9:4	15:382, 384	467, 468
9:5	15:382[c]	467[c]
9:20	17:100	676
9:21	15:36; 17:100[x]	315, 676[x]

9:24	15:282	428
9:26	15:282	428
9:27	15:282	428
10:2	17:106	678
10:3	17:106, 234	678, 732
10:5[o]	14:290–292	255
10:12	17:100	676
10:13	15:36, 102, 104	315, 346, 347
11:35	15:386–388	469
12:1	14:92; 15:102, 104	170, 346, 347
12:2	15:222, 234; 16:348, 370–372	402, 406, 619, 629
12:3	16:238, 374, 378	569, 630, 632
12:6	15:106	348
12:7	17:120	684
12:8	16:340	615
12:9	16:340	615
12:10	15:62, 90	329, 339

Hosea

1:7	14:282; 15:104	252, 347
2:2	16:284	592
2:18	15:216	399
2:21	15:56	327
3:5	16:342	617
4:6	14:142	190
4:10	17:214	725
4:13	17:136	691
4:17	15:390	470
5:13	17:412	804
5:15	15:382, 388	467–468, 469
6:9	17:418	806
7:4	17:290	756
7:5	17:214–216	725
7:11	17:412	804
7:12	17:412[c]	804[c]
7:14	15:358	458
10:8	17:42	653
11:1	16:262	581
11:8	15:382	467
12:1[o]	17:412 [12:2]	804 [12:2]
12:3[o]	14:248 [12:4]	237 [12:4]
12:4	14:248 [12:5]	237 [12:5]
12:7[o]	17:336 [12:8]	775 [12:8]
13:6	17:60	660

13:11	17:102[c]	677[c]
13:14	16:348	619
14:1	15:360	459
14:9	15:72	332

Joel

1:5	15:358	458
2:12	17:104	678
2:13	17:104	678
2:15	17:108	679
2:16	17:108[q]	679[q]
2:28	16:116, 118	523 (twice)
2:29	16:116[q]	523[q]
3:2	16:314	604

Amos

1:3	16:314	604
1:6	17:264[c]	745[c]
1:13	17:406	802
2:4	16:282 [2:1]	591 [2:1]
2:7[o]	17:290 [2:4]	756 [2:4]
2:14[o]	17:410 [2:11]	803 [2:11]
3:6	15:68	330
4:1	17:332	774
4:13	15:36	316
5:7	17:392	796
5:8	15:62	329
5:11	17:332	774
5:14	15:382[c]	468[c]
5:15	15:382	468
5:18	17:54	658
5:21	17:78	668
6:1	17:62	661
6:3	17:62[c]	661[c]
6:5	17:78	668
6:6	17:206	721
6:12	17:392[c]	796[c]
6:13	17:56	659
7:[o,1]	17:418	806
7:10	16:316	605
7:13	16:316[c]	605[c]
8:4	17:332	774
8:5	17:332[c], 336	774[c], 775

8:6	17:334	775
8:11	17:418	806
9:14	16:342–344	617–618
9:15	16:342[c]	617–618[c]

Obadiah

v. 10	16:314	604

Jonah

3:4[o]	14:68 [3:5]	156
3:6[o]	17:104 [3:7], 108[c] [3:7]	678 [3:7], 679[c] [3:7]
3:7	17:104 [3:8]	678 [3:8]
3:8	17:104 [3:9]	678 [3:9]
3:10[o]	14:68[c] [3:11]	156[c]
4:1[o]	17:154[c]	698[c]
4:2[o]	17:154[c]	698[c]
4:3	17:68, 154[c]	663, 698[c]
4:10	15:382	467
4:11	15:382	467

Micah

1:3	14:60[c]	152[c]
2:1	17:332[c]	774[c]
2:2	17:332	774
2:6	17:420	807
2:11	17:420	807
3:2	17:332	774
3:3	17:332[c]	774[c]
3:5	17:418	806
3:6	17:418[c]	806[c]
3:11	17:54, 392, 418	658, 796, 806
4:1	15:282; 16:122[c]	429, 525[c]
4:13	16:314	604
5:2	14:188[c]; 15:280, 282	210[c], 428 (twice)
5:12	17:150	696
6:6	17:74, 78[c]	666, 668[c]
6:7	17:78[x]	668[x]
6:8	17:78[x]	668[x]
6:11	17:336	775
7:3	17:392	796
7:4	17:324	771

Nahum

1:3	14:60[q]	152[q]

Habakkuk

1:12	14:44	143
1:13	14:56	150
1:16	17:60	660
2:2	16:250	575
2:3	16:250[q]	575[q]
2:4	16:30	487
2:12	17:412	804
2:15	17:216	725
2:16	17:216[c]	725[c]
2:18	17:142	693
2:19	17:142	693
3:3	14:60[c]	152[c]

Zephaniah

1:8	17:222	728
1:12	17:62	661
2:1	14:142	190–191
2:2	14:142	190–191
2:3	14:142	190–191
2:8	17:156	699
3:4	17:418	806

Haggai

2:6[o,1]	15:282	429
2:7	15:282 (twice); 16:124	428, 429, 525
2:9	15:282	428

Zechariah

1:3	15:210	397
1:10	15:100	345
1:16	14:112	179
2:8[o]	15:62 [2:12]	329
3:1	14:282; 15:108, 110	252, 348, 349
3:2	14:282	252
3:3	14:282	252
3:7	16:106, 348	518, 619
4:10	15:102	346

5:3	17:330	773
6:12	15:282, 288	428, 432
6:13	15:288, 290	432, 433
7:5	17:104, 108[c]	678, 679[c]
7:9	17:268	747
7:12	15:84	337
8:16	17:296	759
8:19	17:108[c]	679[c]
8:20	16:124	525
8:23	16:344	618
9:9	15:282	428
9:16	17:224[c]	729[c]
9:17	17:224	729
10:4	17:410[c]	803[c]
10:5	17:410	803
10:6	17:410[c]	803[c]
11:13	14:296	257
11:15	17:418	806
11:16	17:418[c]	806[c]
11:17	17:418	806
12:1	15:38, 48	317, 323
12:3	16:314	604
12:4	16:344	618
12:8	14:244	234
12:10	14:298 (twice); 17:82	258 (twice), 670
13:2	17:418	806

Malachi

1:2	14:160 (twice)	198[1]
1:3	14:160 (twice)	198[2]
1:6	17:60	660
1:8	17:116	682
1:11	17:168	704
2:1[3]	17:418	806
2:10	15:4	300
2:11[o]	15:132–134	361
2:13	17:350[c]	782[c]
2:14	17:350	782
2:15	15:132; 17:350[c]	360–361, 782[c]
2:16	15:164	375
3:1	14:240, 290, 298, 300, 348; 15:282, 284	232, 255, 258 (twice), 277, 429, 430
3:5	17:336	775
3:6	14:46	144

3:7	16:282	591–592
3:8	17:116	682
3:9	17:116[x]	682[x]
3:16	17:54[c]	658[c]
3:17	17:54[c]	658[c]
3:18	17:54	658

Apocrypha

TEXT	COLUMBIA EDITION	YALE EDITION
Wisdom 11:17	15:18	306
I Macc. 1:57°	16:256 [1:59, 60]	578 [1:59, 60]
II Macc. 7:28	15:18	306
II Macc. 12:42–45	15:348	455

New Testament

Symbols

[o] Fletcher *omits* this reference.

[c] Milton *cites* this verse but does not quote it.

[q] Milton *quotes* this verse but does not cite it.

[x] Milton quotes this verse but does not give its *exact* location.

New Testament

TEXT	COLUMBIA EDITION	YALE EDITION

Matthew

TEXT	COLUMBIA EDITION	YALE EDITION
1:18	14:362–364, 388[1]; 15:280	283, 293[2], 428
1:20	14:362–364, 388[3]; 15:280	283, 293[4], 427
1:21	15:286	431
1:23	14:258	241
1:25	15:10	303
2:1	17:150[c]	696[c]
2:2	17:150[c]	696[c]
2:5	15:296	435
2:6	15:296	435
2:8	17:318	768
2:13	16:316[c]	605[c]
2:15	16:262	581
2:18	15:18, 222	306–307, 402
3	14:366; 15:304 (twice)	284, 439 (twice)
3:1	16:120[c]	524[c]
3:2	15:300	437
3:5	15:384[c]	468[c]
3:6	15:384; 16:182	468, 549–550
3:7	17:54–56, 324–326	658, 771
3:8	15:382	468
3:11	14:370; 16:186[c]	286, 551[c]
3:12	16:218	563
3:14	16:202[c]	556[c]
3:15	16:186[c]	551[c]
3:16	14:368	285
3:17	14:348; 15:330[q]	277, 449[q]
4:[o]	15:304	439
4:3	15:110	350
4:4[5]	14:358	281

4:6	17:56[c]	658[c]
4:7	17:56, 148	658, 696
4:9	17:242	736
4:10[6]	17:74	666
4:11	15:98	344
4:17	15:288–290; 16:120[c]	432, 524[c]
4:19	17:414	805
5:3	16:66; 17:64	502, 662
5:5	17:284	754
5:7	17:268	747
5:8	16:374	631
5:10	16:316	605
5:11	16:316[c]; 17:162, 240	605[c], 701, 735
5:12	15:336; 16:378	451, 632
5:16	17:10, 166	640, 702
5:17	15:316; 16:140–142	443, 531
5:18	16:368[c]	627[c]
5:20	16:42; 17:198	491, 719
5:22	16:372; 17:208, 286, 314	629, 722, 755, 766
5:24	17:86	671
5:28	15:198; 17:44, 220–222	391, 653, 728
5:29	17:14	642
5:30	17:14[c]	642[c]
5:32	15:134 (twice)	361 (twice)
5:33	17:124, 130[c]	686, 688[c]
5:39	16:300[c]; 17:252	598[c], 740
5:40	16:300[c]; 17:314	598[c], 767
5:42	17:336	775
5:44	17:96, 256 (twice)	675, 742 (twice)
5:45	15:54; 17:102, 256[x]	326, 677, 742[x]
5:48	14:60; 16:18	151, 482
6:[o]	17:88	672
6:1	17:44, 378	653–654, 791
6:2	17:258	742
6:3	17:258[c]	742[c]
6:4	15:54; 17:258[c]	326, 742[c]
6:5	17:92	674
6:6	14:236; 17:86[c], 92	231, 671[c], 673
6:7	17:90[c]	672[c]
6:8	15:54	326
6:9	14:236	231
6:10	15:34; 17:70	315, 664
6:12	17:86, 284	671, 754
6:13	14:226; 15:54, 86	227–228, 326, 338
6:14	17:284	754

6:15	17:256	742
6:16	17:106	678
6:17	17:106	678–679
6:18	17:106	678–679
6:19	17:228	730–731
6:24	17:74[7], 228–230	666[8], 731
6:25	17:226	730
6:26	15:54, 62	326, 329
6:32	15:54	326
6:33	17:82, 228	670, 730
7:1	16:156; 17:310	538, 765
7:3	17:312	765
7:6	17:30, 164	648, 702
7:7	17:80	669 [7:7–10]
7:9	17:80[c]	669[c] [7:7–10]
7:10	17:80[c]	669[c] [7:7–10]
7:11	15:54	326
7:12	16:144; 17:192, 198	532, 716, 718
7:15	16:304	600
7:16	16:304	600
7:21	14:232	230
7:22	15:362–364; 16:222	460, 564
7:23	14:120–122; 16:222–224	182, 564
7:24	16:80	507
7:25	16:80[c]	507[c]
8	17:410	803
8:10	14:134	187
8:11	15:30	312
8:12	16:372 (twice)	629 (twice)
8:16	15:34	314
8:19	17:44	654
8:20	15:304	439
8:21	17:358, 414	784, 805
8:22	17:358[c], 414	784[c], 805
8:29	15:106, 110	348, 349
8:31	15:108–110; 17:102	349, 677
8:32	15:34; 17:102	314, 677
9:2	15:398; 17:158	473, 700
9:3	17:158[c]	700[c]
9:6	14:324	268
9:10	17:14	642
9:11	17:414	805
9:12[o]	17:414[x]	805[x]
9:13	15:350	456
9:15	17:104	677

9:16	16:312, 328	604, 610
9:36	17:414	805
9:37	17:418–420	806
9:38	17:96, 266[c], 418–420	674, 746[c], 806
10:1	14:328; 16:228[c]	269, 566[c]
10:8	15:364; 16:292	460, 596
10:10	16:292	595
10:11	14:130; 16:296	186, 597
10:13[o]	14:130[x]	186[x]
10:14	16:120; 17:414	525, 805
10:15	16:120	525
10:16	16:316; 17:36, 316	605, 651, 767
10:17	16:316; 17:36	605, 651
10:18	15:352	456
10:20	14:370, 372–374	286, 286–287
10:22	16:86[c]	509[c]
10:23	16:316; 17:250	605, 739
10:25	16:316	605
10:28	15:238; 16:372; 17:60, 64, 206, 248	408, 629, 660, 661, 721, 738–739
10:29	15:54, 62	326, 329
10:30	15:62	329
10:32	16:318; 17:160	605, 701
10:33	17:160–162	701
10:37	17:258	743
10:39	17:200	719
10:40	14:380; 17:380, 420	289–290, 792, 806
10:41	14:390; 17:380[c]	293, 792[c]
10:42	17:374, 380[c]	789, 792[c]
11:8	17:222	728
11:10	14:300	259
11:14	14:298	258
11:15	15:354	457
11:21	14:146, 168[c]; 15:96, 352	192, 200[c], 342, 456
11:22	14:168[c]; 16:372	200[c], 629
11:23	14:130, 146[c], 168[c]	186, 192[c], 200[c]
11:25	14:168, 346; 15:4, 392	200, 277, 300, 471
11:26	14:168, 346	200, 277
11:27	14:16, 302, 316, 348, 386; 15:296; 16:6	126, 259, 265, 277, 292, 435, 478
11:28	16:108	519
11:29	16:154; 17:284	537, 754
11:30	16:154	537
12:1	17:194	716
12:4	16:52[c]	496[c]
12:7	17:194	716

12:15	16:316[c]	605[c]
12:18	14:348	277
12:24[9]	14:396[c]; 15:110	296[c], 349
12:25[o]	14:396[c]	296[c]
12:26[o]	14:396[c]	296[c]
12:27[o]	14:396[c]	296[c]
12:28	14:320, 364, 396[c] (twice); 15:6	267, 283, 296[c] (twice), 301
12:29[o]	14:396[c]	296[c]
12:30	14:396[c]; 15:200; 17:152[c]	296[c], 391, 697[c]
12:31	14:394, 396[c]	295, 296[c]
12:32	14:394, 396[c]	295, 296[c]
12:34	16:94; 17:210, 314	512, 723, 766
12:35	17:24, 38–40	646, 652
12:36	15:198; 16:356; 17:210[c], 320	391, 622, 723[c], 769
12:37	16:356; 17:210[c]	622, 723[c]
12:39	16:226	565
12:41	16:226[q], 350	565[q], 620
12:43	15:108 (twice), 110	348, 349, 350
12:44	17:78	668
12:45	15:34	314
12:46	17:276[c]	751[c]
12:50	14:234	230
13:[o]	14:130	186
13:11	14:168	200
13:13	14:170[10]; 15:70	200, 331–332
13:17	16:114	522
13:20	15:362; 17:48	459, 655
13:21	15:362; 17:48	459–460, 655
13:22	17:48	655
13:24	16:218	563
13:25	16:218	563
13:29	16:162	541
13:30	16:162	541[11]
13:41	15:102	346
13:42[12]	16:372 (twice)	629 (twice)
13:43	16:374	630
13:47	16:218	563
13:49	15:234	406
13:52	14:20; 16:266; 17:414	127–128, 584, 805
14:[o,13]	17:128	688
14:4	17:326	771
14:23	17:92	673
14:31	14:322; 17:58	267, 659
15:2	16:160[c], 284	540[c], 592
15:3	16:160[c], 282[c], 284; 17:74	540[c], 591[c], 592, 667

15:5	17:116, 194, 358	682, 716–717, 784
15:8	17:76[c]	667–668[c]
15:9	16:282[c]; 17:76[c]	591[c], 667–668[c]
15:11	15:198	391
15:12	17:14	642
15:13	16:2; 17:14	477, 642
15:14[o]	17:14[x]	642[x]
15:17	17:112	680
15:18	17:44, 112[c]	653, 680[c]
15:19	15:194, 198–200; 17:44, 156[14], 158	389, 391, 653, 699[15], 700
15:26	15:350	456
15:28	14:134	187–188
16:6	16:304	600
16:12	16:304	600–601
16:15	14:352	279
16:16	14:256, 352; 15:258, 392	240, 279, 418, 471
16:17	14:18, 256, 352; 15:392; 16:6	127, 240, 279, 471, 478
16:18	14:352; 16:230	279, 567
16:19	14:352[c]; 16:230[c], 326	279[c], 567[c], 609
16:20	17:164	702
16:23	17:200, 328	720, 771
16:24	17:66	663
16:27	14:266[c], 338; 17:2	245[c], 273, 637
17:5	14:348	277
17:16	16:224	565
17:19[o]	15:364 [17:20]	460 [17:20]
17:21	17:108	679
17:26	17:400	799
17:27	17:400	799
18:6	17:14	642
18:7	15:66; 17:14 (twice)[c]	330, 642 (twice)[c]
18:8	17:14[c]	642[c]
18:10	14:232; 15:100, 102	230, 345, 346
18:11	15:322	447
18:12	17:414	805
18:15	16:334	612
18:16	16:334	612
18:17	16:326, 328, 330	609, 610, 611
18:18	16:230, 326	567, 609
18:19	14:236; 16:230[c], 326; 17:88 (twice)[16]	231, 567[c], 609, 672 (twice)[17]
18:20	14:314; 16:226, 306, 326	265, 566, 601, 609
18:21	17:284	754
18:22	17:284	754
18:23	17:86[c]	671[c]

18:25	17:368	787
18:27	17:318[c]	768[c]
18:32	17:318[c]	768[c]
18:34	17:318[c]	768[c]
18:35	14:226	228
19:3	15:158	372–373
19:4	15:170[18]	377
19:5	15:124 (twice)[19], 134, 154–156	356, 357, 361, 371
19:6	15:156[20]	371
19:8	15:158, 170[21]	372, 377
19:9	15:170[22]	378
19:10	15:176[23]	380
19:11	15:154; 17:16[c], 112	370, 643[c], 681
19:13	16:170	545
19:14	16:170, 172[q]; 17:316	545, 546[q], 767
19:15	16:170[c]	545[c]
19:16	15:358	458
19:17	14:58, 232	150, 229
19:19	17:196[c]	717[c]
19:21	17:16[c]	643[c]
19:22	15:358	458
19:26	14:46	145
19:28	16:228[c], 354, 360	566[c], 622, 625
19:29	15:390; 16:380	470, 632
20:1	15:352[c]	456[c]
20:2	15:352[c]	456[c]
20:3	15:352	456
20:15	17:266	747
20:16	14:116	180
20:20	14:226	228
20:21	14:226; 17:266[c]	228, 746[c]
20:22	17:102	676
20:23	14:226; 16:378	228, 632
20:25	16:234[c]; 17:386	568[c], 795
20:26[o]	17:386 [20:27]	795 [20:27]
20:27	17:386 [20:28]	795 [20:28]
20:28	15:256, 292, 316[24], 322; 16:234[q], 292	417, 434, 444[25], 446, 568[q], 596
21:5	17:284	754
21:7	17:242	736
21:12	14:240	232
21:21	17:58	659
21:30	17:78	668
21:31	14:132	187
21:37	16:120	525

21:38[o]	16:120[q]	525[q]
21:41[o]	16:120[q]	525[q]
21:43	14:154	195
22:8	15:352	456
22:9	15:352; 16:220	456, 563
22:10	15:352; 16:220	456, 563
22:13	16:372	629
22:14	15:364	460
22:21	17:398	799
22:30	16:374	630–631
22:32	16:350	620
22:37	16:144[c]; 17:52[c]	532[c], 657[c]
22:39	16:144[c]	532[c]
22:40	16:144	532
22:43	16:248	574
22:44	15:296, 300	435, 437
23:3	17:78	668
23:5	17:240	735
23:8	15:288	432
23:12	17:236, 238	733, 734
23:15	17:78	668
23:25	17:44	654
23:26	17:44[c]	654[c]
23:34	15:188	386
23:35	15:188	386
23:37	14:154; 15:328, 352	195, 448, 456
24:[o,26]	16:340 (twice)	616 (twice)
24:6	17:250	739
24:12	16:86	509
24:13	16:86; 17:46	509, 655
24:14	16:122	525
24:22	14:96	172
24:24	16:76, 224	506, 564
24:27	16:346	618
24:29	16:346	619
24:30	16:346 (twice)[27]	618, 619[c]
24:31	15:102, 238; 16:354	346, 408, 622
24:35	16:368	628
24:36	14:226, 230, 318; 15:106; 16:338[c]	227, 229, 266, 348, 615[c]
24:42	17:216	726
25[28]	17:62	661
25:1	16:220	563
25:2	16:220	563
25:3	16:96	513
25:6	16:340	615

25:13	17:216[c]	726[c]
25:29	14:170	200
25:30	16:372	629
25:31	15:34; 16:338, 346	315, 614–615, 618
25:32	16:354	622
25:34	16:46, 364; 17:380	493, 626, 792
25:35	14:296; 16:46; 17:380	257, 493, 792
25:36	17:376–378	791
25:40	14:296	257–258
25:41	15:36, 106, 110; 16:364, 370, 372[c]	315, 348, 349, 626, 628, 629–630[c]
25:42	15:200	391
25:45	17:380	792
25:46	16:364	626
26:26	16:190, 200	552, 555
26:27	16:190, 200[c]	552, 555[c]
26:28	16:112, 190	522, 552
26:29	14:226; 16:190, 380	228, 552, 632
26:33	16:232[c]	567[c]
26:35	17:320	768
26:38	15:230	405
26:39	14:228, 328; 15:276; 17:70	229, 269, 425–426, 664
26:41	17:216[c]	726[c]
26:42	14:230[c],[29]; 17:70	229[c], 664
26:53	14:230[30], 15:34	229, 315
26:55	16:324[c]	608[c]
26:61	17:312	766
26:63	17:132	689
26:64	15:312; 17:132	442, 689
26:72	17:126[c]	687[c]
26:74	17:126[c]	687[c]
27:5	17:58, 228	659, 731
27:9	16:276[c]	588[c]
27:46	14:328–330 [27:40]; 15:304, 306	270, 438, 439
27:52	15:244 (twice)[31], 334	412 (twice)[32], 450
27:53	15:244, 334	412, 450
28:2	15:104	347
28:3	15:104	347
28:6	15:314	442–443
28:18	14:318, 332, 392[33]; 15:56, 296	266, 271, 294, 327, 435
28:19	14:332, 370, 374, 390; 15:290, 352; 16:168, 186[q], 220, 232[c], 234, 248	271, 286, 287, 293, 433, 457, 544, 551[q], 563, 567[c], 569, 573
28:20	14:316; 15:290; 16:220, 226, 234[c], 248[c]	265, 433, 563, 566, 569[c], 573[c]

Mark

1:1	14:226[c]	227[c]
1:4	16:182	549
1:10	14:368	285
1:14	15:290	432
1:15	15:386, 404; 16:120[c]	469, 475, 524[c]
1:35	17:94	674
2:27	16:142; 17:174, 194	532, 707, 717
3:4	17:174	707
3:5	17:208	722
3:21	17:34	650
3:22	17:154	698
3:29	17:154	698
3:30	14:396	296
3:35	17:276[c]	751[c]
4:34	17:30	648
5:10	15:108; 17:102[c]	349, 677[c]
5:12	17:102[c]	677[c]
5:13	17:102[c]	677[c]
5:22	16:324	609
6:3	15:304; 16:302[c]	439, 600[c]
6:13[1]	16:216 (twice)	562 (twice)
6:20	15:354	457
7:4	16:182[c]	550[c]
7:7	17:74	667
7:8	16:284[c]; 17:74[c]	592[c], 667[c]
7:9	16:284[c]	592[c]
7:11	17:194[c], 358[c]	717[c], 784[c]
7:12	17:194[c], 358[c]	717[c], 784[c]
7:15	17:112	680–681
7:19	17:112	681
7:22	17:156[c]	699[c]
8:33	17:260	743
8:35	17:200[c]	719[c]
9:23	15:210	397
9:24	14:134; 15:210, 396	188, 397, 472
9:38	16:242	571
9:39	16:242	571
9:42	17:14[c]	642[c]
9:43	16:372	629
9:44[o]	16:370	629
9:49	17:38	651
10:11	15:134	362
10:15	17:316	767
10:16	16:170	545

10:23	17:226	730
10:24	17:226	730
10:25	17:226	730
10:30	16:318	606
10:38	16:184	550
10:42	17:386[c]	795[c]
10:45	15:276	426
11:23	17:58	659
11:24	17:82	669
12:28	14:52[c,2] 198[c]	148[c], 214[c]
12:29	14:52[c], 198[c]	148[c], 214[c]
12:32	14:52, 198[c]	148 [12:42], 214[c]
12:34	14:128, 198	185, 214
12:36	14:366	284–285
12:42	17:20[c]	644[c]
13	16:340	616
13:24[o]	16:346[c]	619[c]
13:25[o]	16:346[c]	619[c]
13:32	14:226, 230, 316–318, 386; 16:338	227, 229, 265–266, 292, 615
13:35	17:216[c]	726[c]
13:37	17:216	726
14:22	16:190[c], 200[3]	552[c], 555[4]
14:23	16:190[c], 200[5]	552[c], 555[6]
14:24	16:112, 190[c], 200[7]	522, 552[c], 555[8]
14:25	16:190[c], 200[9]	552[c], 555[10]
14:26	17:118	683
14:34	15:276	426
14:36	14:230	229
14:39	17:90	672
14:62	15:314	442
16:15	15:352; 16:120, 122, 168	457, 524, 525, 544
16:16	14:112–114; 16:120 (twice)[11], 168, 220[c]	179, 524[12], 525, 544, 564[c]
16:17	15:364; 16:220–222	460, 564
16:18	16:220–222	564
16:19	15:312, 314	442 (twice)
16:20	15:94	341

Luke

1:6	16:46	493
1:9	17:134	690
1:15	15:376	464
1:17	14:298	258
1:19	15:36, 100	315, 345

1:32	14:348; 15:296; 16:360	277, 435, 624–625
1:33	15:296–298; 16:360, 366	435–436, 624–625, 627
1:35	14:364, 388[1]; 15:280	283, 293[2], 428
1:37	14:46	145
1:42	15:280	428
1:46	15:40	318–319
1:47	15:40, 254	318–319, 416
1:68	14:258; 15:254	241, 416
1:69	14:258; 15:254	241, 416
2:6	15:280	428
2:7	15:280, 304	428, 439
2:10	17:204, 266	721, 746
2:13	15:98, 104	344, 347
2:14	15:98	344
2:22	15:280	428
2:24	15:304	439
2:25	14:368	285
2:26	14:368	285
2:37	17:106	678
2:46	16:324	608
2:51	15:304	439
2:52	15:274	425
3:2	16:186[c]	551[c]
3:3	16:186[c]	551[c]
3:11	17:372	789
3:14	17:410	803–804
3:22	14:368	285
3:38	16:50	495
4:1	14:364	284
4:6	17:242[c]	736[c]
4:16	16:324	608
4:17	16:262	582
4:18	14:364; 15:288	284, 432
4:26[o,3]	17:382	792
4:30	16:316[c]	605[c]
4:34	15:110	349
5:29	17:234	732
6:1	16:160[c]	540[c]
6:9	15:200	391
6:23	16:318	606
6:26	17:240	735
6:27	17:256[c]	742[c]
6:30	17:344	779
6:35	17:336	775
6:36	14:58	150

6:38	17:344	779
7:14	15:236	407
7:29	16:186[c]; 17:420[c]	551[c], 807[c]
7:30	14:114; 15:328, 352; 16:186[c]; 17:420	179, 448, 456, 551[c], 807
7:40[o]	16:48[c]	493–494[c]
7:47	16:48	493–494
7:50	16:48	494
8:2	15:96; 16:160[c]	343, 541[c]
8:3	16:160[c]	541[c]
8:10	16:260	580
8:13	15:362; 16:96	460, 513
8:18	17:420	806–807
8:30	15:34	314
8:31	15:108	349
8:41	16:324	609
9:20	14:352	279
9:23	16:4	478
9:26	15:34, 96; 17:162	315, 343, 701
9:48	17:64	662
9:54	17:154	698
9:62	14:128[4]; 17:48[5]	185[6], 655[7]
10:7	16:296	597
10:8	16:296	597
10:13	14:130, 146	186, 192
10:18	15:34, 108	314, 348
10:20	14:92; 16:226	170, 565
10:22	15:288	432
10:25	16:106[c]	518[c]
10:26	16:256	578
10:28	16:106[c]	518[c]
10:31	15:64; 17:264[c]	329, 745[c]
10:32	17:264[c]	745[c]
10:33	17:268	747
10:36	17:254	741
10:37	17:254	741
11:1	14:236	231
11:2	14:236	231
11:5	17:86[c]	671[c]
11:7	16:94	512
11:13	14:370–372, 392; 15:354, 356	286, 295, 457 (twice)
11:15	15:110	349
11:20	14:320, 364, 396	267, 283, 296
11:23	15:200	391
11:27	17:276[c]	751[c]

11:28	14:22	129
11:38	16:182[c]	550[c]
11:40	17:78	668
11:41	17:374, 380	789, 792
11:42	17:78[c]	668[c]
11:52	16:266	584
11:53	17:312[c]	766[c]
11:54	17:312	766
12:2	17:62	661
12:3	17:62[c]	661[c]
12:4	16:318	605
12:5	16:318[c]	605[c]
12:12	16:118[c]	524[c]
12:14	16:334	612
12:15	17:228	731
12:19[o]	17:62	661
12:32	14:100, 104	173, 176
12:33	16:378; 17:380	632, 792
12:37	17:216	726
12:45	17:62	661
12:47	14:130; 16:372	186, 629
12:48	14:130; 16:372	186, 629
12:50	16:184[c]	550[c]
12:56	17:36	650–651
12:57	17:36	650–651
13:5	14:144	192
13:14	16:324	609
13:15	17:174	707
13:16	17:174	707
13:24	14:172	201
13:25	14:172	201
13:26	17:276[c]	751[c]
13:27	16:370	628
13:28	16:370	628
13:31	17:248[c]	739[c]
13:32	17:248, 326	739, 771
14:1	17:268	747
14:5	17:174	707
14:9	17:364[c]	786[c]
14:10	17:364	786
14:12	17:372, 380[c]	789, 792[c]
14:13	17:372, 378, 380[c]	789, 791, 792[c]
14:14	17:372[c], 380	789[c], 792
14:15	16:380	632–633
14:24	14:172	201

14:26	17:260	743
14:31	17:406	802
14:33	17:52	657
15:10	15:98; 17:266	344, 746
16	15:242	411
16:9	17:372	789
16:10	15:200	392
16:16	16:124	526
16:19	17:234	733
16:22	15:30	312
16:23	16:370, 372	628, 629
16:26	16:372	629
16:28	16:372	629
16:29	16:250, 258	575–576, 578
16:31	16:224–226	565
17:3	17:284	754
17:4	17:284	754
17:5	16:16	482
17:7	17:366	787
17:8	17:366	787
17:9	17:366	787
17:10	17:16, 22, 366[c]	642, 645, 787[c]
17:21	15:298	436
17:26	16:340	615
17:28[o]	16:340[q]	615[q]
18:1	17:94	674
18:2	17:86[c], 240, 296	671[c], 735, 759
18:8	16:342	616–617
18:9	17:86	671
18:13	17:90	673
19:3	14:134	188
19:7	17:14	642
19:8	17:20[c], 312	644[c], 766
19:9	14:134	188
19:27	15:300	437
19:42	14:172	201
20:5	17:42	653
20:6	17:42[c]	653[c]
20:18	17:14	642
20:35	15:222, 226	402, 403
20:36	15:34, 226; 16:54	314, 403, 497
20:37	15:222	402
21	16:340	616
21:4	17:374	789
21:18	16:318	605

21:19	16:318[c]; 17:66	605[c], 663
21:24	16:344	618
21:25	16:346	619
21:26	16:346	619
21:27	16:346[c]	618[c]
21:28	16:338	614
21:34	16:340; 17:214	615, 725
21:35	16:340	615
21:36	17:216	726
22:7	16:198	555
22:8	16:198	555
22:11	16:198	555
22:12	16:198	555
22:19	16:190	552
22:20	16:112, 190, 200	522, 552, 555
22:25	17:388[c]	795[c]
22:29	14:230, 318; 16:360	229, 266, 625
22:30	14:340; 16:354[c], 360–362, 380	274, 622[c], 625, 633
22:32	15:392; 16:76, 86[c], 232	471, 505, 509[c], 567
22:35	16:296	597
22:43	14:328; 15:302	269–270, 438
22:51	17:256	742
23:34	14:228; 15:326; 17:96, 256	229, 448, 675, 742
23:43	15:30, 242–244, 308[q]	312, 411–412, 440[q]
23:46	14:230, 330; 15:244–246[8], 276	229, 270, 412, 426
24:5	15:234–236	407
24:26	15:308, 310	440, 441
24:27	16:116	523
24:32	15:290	432–433
24:36	17:186[c]	712[c]
24:39	14:40; 15:276	140, 426
24:44	16:116	523
24:45	15:290; 16:258	432–433, 579
24:47	16:120[c]	524[c]
24:49	14:372	286
24:51	15:312, 314	442, 443
24:52	17:204	721

John

1:1	14:180, 252, 306, 336; 15:258	206, 238–239[q], 261, 272, 418
1:2	14:180[c], 254	206[c], 239
1:3	14:180[c], 204; 15:6	206[c], 217, 301
1:4	14:16–18	126
1:5	15:206	395

1:9	14:18, 148; 15:288, 348, 354	126, 193, 432, 455, 457
1:10	15:6, 290	301, 433
1:11	14:114, 156–158	179, 197
1:12	14:114–116, 156–158; 15:366, 400, 404; 16:50	179–180, 197, 461, 474, 475, 495
1:13	14:188; 15:366; 17:364	210, 461, 786
1:14	14:188, 336[1]; 15:258	210, 272[2], 418
1:16	15:288	432
1:17	15:260, 286, 288; 16:100, 152	419, 431, 432, 515, 536
1:18	14:30, 188, 198, 248, 252, 336, 15:288	133, 210, 214, 237, 239, 272, 432
1:29	14:350; 16:168	277, 543
1:32	14:370	285
1:33	14:300, 350, 370; 16:186	259, 277, 285, 551 [1:23]
1:34	14:350	277
1:48[o]	14:314 [1:49]	264 [1:49]
1:49	14:314 [1:50], 352	264 [1:50], 279
1:50	14:314, 352	264, 279[q]
1:51	15:352[q]	279[q]
2:14	17:152[c]	697[c]
2:16	14:236–238; 17:418	231, 806
2:19	14:236; 15:310	231 [2:9], 441
2:21	14:242[c]	233[c]
2:23	14:334	271
2:24	14:316, 334	265, 271
2:25	14:316	265
3:2	17:164	702
3:3	15:366	461
3:5	15:366, 368 (twice); 16:184, 202	461 (twice), 462, 550, 557
3:6	15:50, 194, 366 (twice); 17:364	324, 389, 461, 462, 786
3:8	14:388	293
3:13	14:314; 15:258, 278	264, 418, 427
3:14	16:102[c]	516[c]
3:15	15:404; 16:102[c], 120	475, 516[c], 524
3:16	14:104, 114, 188, 224, 270[c]; 15:252, 284, 318, 320[x]; 16:70, 102[c], 120[c]	175, 179, 210, 226, 247[c], 416, 431, 445, 445–446[x], 504, 516[c], 524[c]
3:17	15:284, 318, 324	431, 445, 447
3:18	14:154, 188[c]; 15:404	196, 210[c], 475
3:19	14:154–156; 16:120–122; 17:328	196, 525, 771–772
3:21	17:4	638
3:26	17:266[c]	746[c]
3:31	14:262, 316, 350; 15:258	243, 265, 277–278, 418–419
3:32	14:262, 316, 350	243, 265, 277–278
3:33	14:316; 15:400	265, 473

3:34	14:316; 15:260, 284	265, 419, 431
3:35	14:302, 302–304, 334	259, 260, 272
3:36	14:334	272
4:[o]	16:204	557
4:2	16:246	573 [4:12]
4:10	16:192	553
4:14	16:80, 192	507, 553
4:20	16:284	592
4:21	14:198; 16:232; 17:168	214, 568, 704
4:22	14:376	288
4:23	14:238 [4:21, 23]; 15:298; 16:234; 17:168	231 [4:21–23], 436, 568, 704
4:24	14:40; 15:298	140, 436
4:25	15:288	432
4:41	15:396	472
4:42	16:280[c]	590[c]
4:53[o]	15:396	472
5:4	14:320	267
5:11	17:174[c]	707[c]
5:18	14:186[c], 344	209[c], 276
5:19	14:318, 344	266, 276
5:20	14:316, 320	265, 266
5:21	14:320; 15:372	266, 463
5:22	14:318, 324, 330, 332; 16:354	266, 268, 271 (twice), 622
5:23	14:330, 332	271 (twice)
5:24	14:334	271
5:25	15:372	463
5:26	14:54, 314	149, 264
5:27	16:354	622
5:28	15:230; 16:350	405, 620
5:29	15:230; 16:350	405, 620
5:30	14:318, 344	266, 276
5:34	15:328	448
5:36	14:320	266
5:37	14:30, 248–250, 252	133, 237, 239
5:39	16:106[c], 114, 250–252, 258	518[c], 523, 576, 578
5:40	15:328	448
5:41	17:238	734
5:43	14:318	266
5:44	17:238	734
5:45	14:332	271
5:46	16:116	523
6:[o]	16:192[3], 204	553[4], 557
6:4	16:192	553
6:12	17:230	731

6:15	17:242	736
6:27	14:224; 15:284	226, 431
6:29	14:224; 15:402; 16:30	226, 474, 487
6:32	14:232; 15:324	230, 447
6:33	16:190	552
6:35	15:404–406; 16:190–192, 192	475, 552–553, 553
6:36	15:324	447
6:37	15:332, 344; 16:76	449–450, 454, 505
6:38	14:230, 344	229, 276
6:39	15:332[c]; 16:350[c]	449[c], 620[c]
6:40	14:334; 16:350[c]	272, 620[c]
6:44	14:320–322; 15:344, 394	267, 454, 471
6:45	14:18; 15:394; 16:6	127, 471, 478
6:46	14:18[c], 30, 336[5]	127[c], 133, 272[6]
6:47	15:404; 16:70[c]	475, 504[c]
6:50[7]	16:192 (twice)	553 (twice)
6:51	15:318; 16:80, 192	445, 507, 553
6:53	16:192[c]	553[c]
6:54	16:192[c]	553[c]
6:55	16:192[c]	553[c]
6:56	16:58, 192	499, 553
6:57	14:204, 314; 16:192	217, 264, 553
6:58	16:192[c], 194	553 (twice)[8]
6:63	16:192	553
6:65	14:232	230
6:66	15:362; 17:164	460, 702
6:69	14:352	279
6:70	14:98	172
7:1	17:250	739
7:5	17:276[c]	751[c]
7:7	16:18; 17:326	482, 771
7:14	16:324[c]; 17:80	608[c], 668
7:16	14:318	266
7:17	14:24, 232; 16:304	129, 230, 601
7:18	14:232; 16:304	230, 601
7:22	16:166[c]	543[c]
7:23	16:166[c]; 17:174	543[c], 707
7:28	14:58, 344	151, 276
7:29	14:306	261
7:39	14:370; 16:118	286, 524
8:[o,9]	16:278	589
8:7	16:334	612–613
8:9	17:42	653
8:11	16:334	612
8:12	15:290	433

8:16	14:400	298
8:18	14:400	298
8:26	14:316	265
8:28	14:206[c], 316, 320	218[c], 265, 266
8:29	14:344–346	276
8:31	14:24; 16:86, 90[q], 152	129, 510, 511[q], 536
8:32	14:24; 16:152	129, 536
8:34	15:206	395
8:35	16:76	506
8:36	16:152	536
8:38	14:316	265
8:39	17:364	786
8:41	14:198 [8:41, 54]	214 [8:41–54]
8:42	14:206[c], 318, 346	218[c], 266, 276
8:43	14:170; 15:206	200, 395
8:44	14:170 (twice); 15:34, 96, 110, 180; 16:264; 17:296	201 (twice), 315, 343, 349, 383, 583, 759
8:46	14:170	201
8:47	14:170	201
8:49	14:346	276
8:50	14:340, 346	274, 276
8:51	16:20	483
8:54	14:198 [8:41, 54], 346	214 [8:41–54], 276
8:56	15:396	472
8:58	15:278	427
8:59	16:316[c]	605[c]
9:3	15:390	470
9:16	17:176	708 [10:16]
9:22	16:330[c]	611[c]
9:29	14:18	127
9:31	17:84, 100	671, 676
9:32	14:44	144
9:34	16:330[c]	611[c]
9:35	14:352	279
9:36	14:352	279
9:37	14:352–354	279
9:38	14:352–354	279
9:39	17:32	649
9:41	14:148	193
10:10	17:418	806
10:12	16:302	599
10:13	16:302	599
10:14	16:64	501
10:15	15:256	417
10:16	15:320; 16:64, 122	446, 501, 525

10:18	14:318; 15:256, 310	266, 417, 441
10:20	17:34	650
10:21	15:94	341
10:24	14:346	276
10:25	14:170, 346	201, 276
10:26	14:170 (twice)	201 (twice)
10:27	14:170	201
10:28	15:300; 16:76	436, 506
10:29	14:210, 342–344; 16:76	219, 275–276, 506
10:30	14:208	219
10:32	14:320	266
10:34	14:252; 16:100	238, 516
10:35	14:184[c], 194–196, 252	207[c], 213, 238
10:36	14:184, 210, 252; 15:284	207, 219, 238, 431
10:38	14:210	220
10:41	16:224	565
11:7	17:250[c]	739[c]
11:8	17:250	739
11:11	15:234	406–407
11:13	15:234	406–407
11:22	14:320, 354	266, 279
11:24	14:100[c]	173[c]
11:25	14:334–336; 15:222; 16:350	272, 402, 620
11:26	14:334–336, 354	272, 279
11:27	14:334–336, 354	272, 279
11:41	14:320	266 [10:41]
11:43	15:234	406–407
11:52	16:60	499
11:53	17:250[c]	739[c]
11:54	16:316[c]; 17:250	605[c], 739
12:2	17:234	732
12:3	16:160[c]; 17:234	540–541[c], 732–733
12:6	17:330[c]	773[c]
12:10	17:30	649
12:25	17:200	719
12:27	14:230	229
12:31	15:108	348
12:32	15:334	450
12:34	14:148[c]	193[c]
12:35[o]	14:148	193
12:36[o]	14:148	193
12:37[o]	14:148[c]	193[c]
12:38[o]	14:148[c]	193[c]
12:39	14:148[c], 172[c]; 15:70	193[c], 201[c], 331
12:40	14:148[c], 172[c]; 15:70 (twice)	193[c], 201[c], 331, 332

12:41	14:148[c], 250, 340	193[c], 237, 274
12:42	14:334; 16:330[c]; 17:164, 238[c]	271, 611[c], 702, 734[c]
12:43	17:152[c], 238	697[c], 734
12:44	14:334; 15:402	272, 474
12:47[o]	15:324 [12:4]	447 [12:4]
12:48	14:156; 16:356	196, 623
12:49	14:318	266
12:50	14:318	266
13:3	14:302	259
13:8	14:114; 17:72	179, 664
13:18	14:322	267
13:20	14:380, 390; 17:420[c]	290, 293, 806[c]
13:23	14:252–254	239
13:29	17:372	789
13:31	14:340	274
13:34	17:270[c]	748[c]
13:35	16:226; 17:270[x]	565–566, 748[x]
14:1	14:224, 334; 15:402	226, 272, 474
14:2	14:228; 15:32, 222, 334	229, 312, 402, 450
14:3	15:32, 222, 242, 334	312, 402, 410, 450
14:4	15:334	450
14:6	15:256, 294	418, 434
14:8	14:264	244
14:9	14:264	244
14:10	14:210–212, 320	220, 267
14:12	14:320; 15:312	267, 442
14:13	15:294 (twice); 17:82	434, 435, 669
14:14	17:82[c]	669[c]
14:15	17:70	664
14:16	14:202, 328, 370, 372	216, 269, 285, 286
14:17	14:370, 372; 15:320; 16:94	285, 286, 446, 513
14:20	14:212; 16:56	220, 498
14:21	14:212; 17:70[c]	220, 664[c]
14:23	14:324, 382, 386[q]; 16:56; 17:70[c]	268, 291, 292[q], 498, 664[c]
14:24	14:318	266
14:26	14:370, 372; 16:118	285, 286, 524
14:28	14:210, 342–344; 15:314	219, 275–276, 443
14:31	14:344	276
15:1	16:2	477
15:2	16:2, 16, 82	477, 481, 507
15:4	16:10	480
15:5	16:10; 17:6	480, 639
15:6	14:114; 16:82	179, 507–508
15:8	14:232	230
15:9	15:286	431

15:10	14:114, 346; 16:74, 82	179, 276, 505, 508
15:11	16:74	505
15:12	17:270	748
15:13[o]	17:270[x]	748[x]
15:15	14:316; 15:288	265, 432
15:16	14:92, 238, 322	169, 231, 267
15:18	16:18, 318	482, 605
15:19	14:322; 15:320; 16:18[c], 318[c]	267, 446, 482[c], 605[c]
15:20	16:318[c]	605[c]
15:22	14:148; 15:346	193, 454
15:24	15:96; 17:52	342, 657
15:26	14:358[10], 370, 372	281[11], 285, 286
16:2	17:30	649
16:3	17:30	649
16:7	14:370, 372; 15:334	285, 286, 450
16:8	14:372	286
16:12	16:270, 328	586, 610
16:13	14:328, 370, 372, 382; 16:8, 270; 17:8[12]	269, 285, 286, 290, 478, 586, 640[13]
16:14	14:372, 386	286, 292
16:15	14:304, 340, 366, 372	260, 274, 284, 286
16:23	14:238; 17:82	231[14], 669
16:25	14:346	276
16:27	14:354	279
16:30	14:316, 354	265, 279
16:31	14:354	279
16:33	15:300, 396	437, 473
17:1	17:100	676
17:2	14:100, 318, 322	173, 266, 267
17:3	14:40, 52, 200, 272[c], 354, 378; 15:394	140, 148, 215, 248[c], 272, 288, 472
17:4	14:232	230
17:5	14:180–182, 306, 336; 15:314; 17:100	206, 261, 272, 443, 676
17:6	14:100, 340	173, 274
17:7	14:340, 354	274, 279
17:8	14:354	279
17:9	14:304; 15:294, 326; 17:98	260, 434, 448, 675
17:10	14:304, 340	260, 274
17:11	14:324; 17:270	268, 748
17:12	14:114, 324	179, 268
17:14	16:18	482
17:15	14:324; 16:76	268, 506
17:17	15:368 (twice)	461, 462
17:18	14:328	269

17:20	14:114; 15:400–402	179, 474
17:21	14:212, 354; 16:56	220, 279, 498
17:22	14:212; 15:334; 16:56, 66	220, 450, 498, 502
17:23	14:212; 16:56	220, 498
17:24	14:336	272–273
18:28	17:396[c]	798[c]
18:29	17:396[c]	798[c]
18:36	15:298; 17:396[15]	436, 799[16]
18:37	15:288; 17:326	432, 771
19:11	15:200	391
19:36	16:168	543
19:37	14:298	258
20:17	14:200, 254–256, 346	215, 240, 276
20:21	14:328 (twice); 16:228[c]	269 (twice), 566[c]
20:22	14:328, 356, 370, 372; 16:228[c], 326	269, 281, 285, 286, 566[c], 609
20:23	16:230, 326	567, 609
20:26	17:186	712
20:28	14:254	239
20:29	14:256; 15;398; 16:226	240, 473, 565
20:31	14:354; 16:252	279–280, 576
21:3	17:186	712
21:4	17:186[c]	712[c]
21:15	16:230[c]	567[c]
21:17	14:316; 15:274	265, 425

Acts

1:2	14:364	284
1:3	15:290	433
1:5	14:370; 16:186 (twice)[c]	286, 551 (twice)[c]
1:7	14:318; 15:54; 16:338–340; 17:34	266, 326, 615, 650
1:8	16:118	524
1:9	15:312	442
1:11	16:338	615
1:16	14:366	285
1:18	17:58	659
1:23	16:290	594
1:24	14:54[1]; 17:134	150[2], 690
1:26	16:214[c]; 17:134	561[c], 690
2:1	15:298; 16:118[c]	436, 524[c]
2:2	14:370, 372	285–286, 286
2:3	14:370, 372	285–286, 286
2:4	14:370, 372, 386	285–286, 286, 292
2:5	16:308[c]	602[c]

2:13	17:312	766
2:14	17:312[c]	766[c]
2:15	17:312[c]	766[c]
2:16	16:118[c]	523[c]
2:17	16:118[c]	523[c]
2:18	16:118[c]	523[c]
2:23	14:64, 90; 15:66	154, 169, 330
2:24	15:310	441
2:27	15:230	405
2:28	14:90–92; 15:230	169, 405
2:29	15:220	402
2:30	15:258, 278	419, 427
2:31	15:230	405
2:32	14:372	286
2:33	14:298, 370, 372; 15:310	258, 285–286, 286, 441
2:34	15:220	402
2:36	14:202[c], 204	216[c], 217
2:38	14:382, 390; 16:118	290, 294, 524
2:39	15:344; 16:120[c], 174, 176[q]	454, 524[c], 546–547, 547[q]
2:40	16:120[c]	524[c]
2:41	16:120[c], 176	524[c], 547
2:42	16:204, 220, 284–286; 17:88, 188[c]	557, 563, 593, 672, 713[c]
2:46	16:204; 17:188[c]	557, 713[c]
3:6	14:328; 17:374	269, 789
3:13	14:338	273
3:19	15:382	468
3:21	14:44; 15:314; 16:380	144, 443, 632
3:22	15:288	432
3:23	16:122	525
4:10	14:272[c]	248[c]
4:11	14:272[c]	248[c]
4:12	15:256	418
4:16	16:226	565
4:17	16:226[c]	565[c]
4:19	14:20; 17:70, 400	127, 664, 800
4:20	16:94	512
4:24	14:224; 15:4; 17:88	227, 300, 672
4:27	15:4, 56	300, 327
4:28	14:64; 15:80	154, 335
4:29[o]	17:70	664
4:34	17:20[c]	644[c]
5	17:300	761
5:3	14:380; 15:110	289, 349
5:4	14:380; 16:334; 17:20[c]	289, 612, 644[c]
5:9	14:380	290

5:30	14:234–236; 15:310	231, 441
5:31	14:234–236[3], 324 (twice), 326, 15:310, 378	231[4], 268 (twice), 269, 441, 466
5:32	14:382; 16:274	290, 587
5:39	17:396	798
5:41	16:318	605
6:2	16:206[c]	558[c]
6:3	16:288	594
6:5	16:288[c], 290	594[c], 594
6:6	16:214[c]	561[c]
6:7	14:24	129
7:9	17:266[c]	746[c]
7:30	14:278	251
7:37	15:288	432
7:38	14:278; 15:286	251, 431
7:51	14:278; 15:328, 352; 17:48, 152[c]	251, 448, 456, 655, 697[c]
7:55	15:314	442
7:59	14:332; 15:246	271, 412–413
7:60	14:324; 15:222; 17:96	268, 402, 675
8:1	16:288[c]	594[c]
8:2	17:260	744
8:4	16:242, 316[c]	571, 605[c]
8:12	16:182, 288	549, 594
8:13	15:362	460
8:14	16:228[c]	567[c]
8:17	16:214[c]	561[c]
8:18	15:362	460
8:20	16:298; 17:98	598, 675–676
8:21	15:362	460
8:27	16:308[c]	602[c]
8:28	16:258	578
8:36	16:168	544
8:37	14:354; 16:168, 176	280, 544, 547
8:38	16:288	594
9:4	14:296	258
9:5	14:296	258
9:10	16:246[c]	573[c]
9:14	14:332	271
9:18	16:246[c]	573[c]
9:31	17:394	797
9:34	14:328	269
10:°	17:410	803
10:2	17:380[c]	792[c]
10:3	17:380[c]	792[c]
10:4	17:380	792
10:9	17:94	674

10:13	16:160[c]; 17:112	540[c], 681
10:15	17:112	681
10:16	14:272[c]	248[c]
10:23	16:246	573
10:26	17:144	694
10:34	14:126, 136[c]; 16:122	184, 188[c], 525
10:35	14:126, 136[c]; 16:120 [10:34], 122	184, 188[c], 525 (twice)[5]
10:38	14:362, 364	283, 284
10:40	15:310	441
10:42	16:338	615
10:43	15:328; 16:28	449, 486–487
10:44	16:202	556
10:45	16:246	573
10:48	16:246	573
11:2	16:228[c]	567[c]
11:16	14:370	286
11:17	16:182	549
11:18	15:378	466
11:19	16:242	571
11:20[o]	16:242[q]	571[q]
11:21[o]	16:242[q]	571[q]
11:22[o]	16:242[q]	571[q]
11:23[o]	16:242[q]	571[q]
12:12	17:88	672
12:15	15:102	346
12:23	17:64	662
13	14:136 (twice)[6]	188 (twice)
13:2	14:386; 16:240, 290; 17:108	292, 570, 595, 679
13:3	16:290; 17:108[q]	595, 679[q]
13:5	16:324	608–609
13:10	17:326	771
13:15	16:240–242, 324 (twice)[7]	571, 609 (twice)[8]
13:32	14:182[c], 364; 15:310, 314	206[c], 284, 441, 443
13:33	14:182, 364; 15:310, 314	206–207, 284, 441, 443
13:34	15:310 (twice)	441 (twice)
13:39	16:30	487
13:46	14:126[c], 148, 154; 15:352	184[c], 193, 195, 456
13:48	14:118[c], 124, 126[9]	181[c], 184, 184 [13:46]
13:51	17:414	805
14:6	16:316[c]	605[c]
14:14	17:152[c]	697[c]
14:15	15:14; 17:144	305, 694
14:16	14:148; 15:66, 352; 16:104	193, 330, 456, 518
14:17	14:24, 148–150; 15:58, 348; 16:104; 17:234	130, 193, 327, 455, 518, 733
14:22	15:390	470

14:23	16:290, 306; 17:108	594, 601–602, 679
15	16:328	610
15:2	16:228[c], 310[c]	566[c], 603[c]
15:5	16:136[c]	530[c]
15:6	16:228[c], 286[c]	566[c], 594[c]
15:7	16:228[c]	566[c]
15:9	15:328, 376	449, 465
15:10	16:110, 124, 136, 280	519–520, 526, 530, 590
15:11	16:110	519–520
15:12	16:312[c]	603[c]
15:18	14:62 [15:28], 64 [15:28], 120	154 (twice), 182 [15:8]
15:19	16:228[c], 280[c]	566[c], 590[c]
15:20	17:142	693
15:22	16:290, 312[c]	594, 603[c]
15:23	16:228[c], 312[c]	566[c], 603[c]
15:24	16:136	530
15:25	16:228[c]	566[c]
15:28	14:370; 16:160[c], 280[c], 310	286, 540[c], 590[c], 603
15:29	16:160; 17:142	540, 693
15:38	17:208[c]	722[c]
15:39	17:208	722
16:3	16:328[c]	610[c]
16:4	16:286[c]	594[c]
16:6	15:350	456
16:7	15:350	456
16:9	15:350	456
16:13	17:88, 190	672, 713
16:14	14:138[c]; 15:290, 354	189[c], 433, 457
16:31	14:258; 16:182	241, 549
16:32	16:182	549
16:33	16:182	549
16:34	14:258 [16:24]; 16:182	241, 549
16:37	17:252	740
17:2	17:190	713
17:11	16:116, 258, 304	523, 578, 601
17:16	17:136, 152[c]	691, 697[c]
17:17	17:152[c]	697[c]
17:18	17:34	650
17:24	15:14	305
17:25	15:58	327
17:26	15:48, 184	323, 385
17:27	14:24; 15:352; 16:104	130, 456, 518
17:28	14:24[c]; 15:58; 16:104[c]	130[c], 327, 518[c]
17:29	14:38[10]; 17:138–140	137[11], 692
17:30	15:324, 352; 16:104	447, 456, 518

17:31	15:324; 16:338, 354	447, 615, 622
17:32	17:34–36	650
18:3	16:302[c]; 17:190	600[c], 713
18:4	16:302[c]; 17:190	600[c], 713
18:6	17:156[12], 414	699[13], 805
18:8	16:182	549
18:15	17:396	798
18:18	17:110	680
18:24	16:202[c], 242, 258	556[c], 571, 578
18:25	16:202[c], 242	556[c], 571–572
18:26	16:202[c]	556[c]
18:28	16:258	579
19:1	16:186[c]	551[c]
19:2[14]	16:186 (twice)	551 (twice)
19:3	14:390; 16:120[c], 188[c]	294, 525[c], 552[c]
19:4	15:386; 16:120[c], 186[c]	469, 525[c], 551[c]
19:5	16:186[c], 188	551[c], 552
19:6	16:214[c]	561[c]
19:8	17:326	771
19:9	17:326[c]	771[c]
19:13	17:132	690
19:18	15:384	468
19:19	17:34	650
20:7	16:204–206; 17:188	557, 712
20:17	16:286	593
20:20	16:236	569
20:21	15:386; 16:120[c], 236	469, 525[c], 569
20:27	14:22	128
20:28	14:260[15], 270, 386–388; 15:254, 292, 320; 16:286	241–242[16], 247, 292, 417, 434, 446, 593
20:29	16:290, 300	595, 598
20:30	16:290–292	595
20:33	16:300	598
20:34	16:292–294	596
20:35	16:292, 292–294; 17:114	596 (twice), 681
20:36	17:88	672
21:5	17:88	672
21:8	16:288	594
21:13	16:318	605
21:20	17:272	749
21:23	17:110, 272[x]	680, 749[x]
21:26	16:328[c]	610[c]
22:16	16:184	550
23:1	17:40	652
23:3	17:326	771

23:4[o]	17:400 [23:3]	799 [23:3]
23:5[o]	17:400[x]	799[x]
23:6	15:222	402
23:17	17:410	804
24:14	14:14, 22	124, 129
24:15	15:400; 16:348	474, 619
24:16	14:22 [24:6]; 17:40	129, 652
24:21	15:224	402 [Luke 24:21]
24:25	17:42	653
26:6	15:224; 16:348–350	402 [Luke 26:6–8], 619–620
26:7	15:224; 16:348[c]	402 [Luke 26:6–8], 619[c]
26:8	15:224; 16:348–350	402 [Luke 26:6–8], 619–620
26:11	17:156[c]	699[c]
26:18	15:206, 382; 16:28	395, 468, 487
26:20	15:382	468
26:22	16:116	523
26:23	16:116[c]	523[c]
26:24	17:36	650
26:28	15:354	457
27:24	14:68	156
27:31	14:68	156
27:35	17:160	700
28:4	17:312	765
28:25	14:366, 382	285, 290

Romans

1:1	14:18	127
1:3	15:258	419
1:4	14:182, 364; 15:310, 314	207, 283–284, 441–442, 443
1:7	14:226[c]; 16:254[c]	227[c], 577[c]
1:8	14:226[c], 238; 17:96[c]	227[c], 231, 675[c]
1:9	14:238; 17:96	231, 675
1:10	17:96[c]	675[c]
1:14	16:248	573
1:15	16:254[c]	577[c]
1:16	16:120 (twice), 202	524 (twice), 557
1:17	16:120 (twice)[c]	524 (twice)[c]
1:18	15:346	454
1:19	14:24–26; 15:208, 346, 348; 16:100, 108	130, 396, 454, 455, 516, 519
1:20	14:24–26[c], 38[1]; 15:14, 208, 346	130[c], 137[2], 305, 396, 454
1:21	14:172; 17:60	201–202, 660
1:22	17:32	649
1:23	14:46; 17:140	144, 692

1:24	14:172; 15:76; 17:140[c]	201–202, 334, 692[c]
1:25	14:262	243
1:26	14:172; 15:208	201–202, 395
1:28	15:70, 84	332, 337
1:29	17:312	766
1:30	17:312	766
1:31	17:278[c]	751[c]
1:32	15:196, 208; 16:100; 17:278	390, 396, 516, 751
2:4	15:80, 378; 16:104[c]; 17:56	336, 466, 517[c], 658
2:5	15:80, 378	336, 466
2:6	15:336; 16:44	451, 492
2:7	15:336	451
2:8	16:372	629
2:9	15:216; 16:372	399, 629
2:10	14:126[c]	184[c]
2:11	14:126	184
2:12	15:180; 16:356	382, 623
2:13	14:22; 17:2	129, 637
2:14	14:26, 126; 15:210; 16:100, 356	130, 184, 397, 516, 623
2:15	14:26; 15:208, 348, 358; 16:100, 356–358[q]; 17:40, 42	130, 396, 455, 458, 516, 623[q], 652, 653
2:16	14:330; 16:354, 358[q]	270, 622, 623[q]
2:20[3]	14:22	128
2:24	17:166	703
2:25	16:166	543
2:29	16:62	500
3:2	16:250[c]	574[c]
3:4	14:58	151
3:9	15:196	390
3:19	15:196, 202–204; 16:108	390, 394, 519
3:20	16:30, 106	487, 518
3:21	16:30, 116, 124	487, 523, 526
3:22	15:328; 16:30–32, 124[c]	449, 487, 526[c]
3:23	15:192, 328[4]; 16:30–32	388, 449[5], 487
3:24	15:328[6]; 16:24, 36[c]	449[7], 485, 489[c]
3:25	15:252, 254, 256, 284, 292–294, 326, 328[8], 330; 16:24–26	416, 417 (twice), 431, 434, 448, 449[9], 449, 485
3:26	16:24–26	485–486
3:27	16:32, 36[c], 40 (twice), 132	487–488, 489[c], 491 (twice), 528
3:28	16:32, 36[c], 36–38, 40 (twice)[10]	487–488, 489[c], 490, 491 (twice)[11]
3:30	14:52; 16:32	148, 488
3:31	16:142	531
4:1	16:40	491
4:2	16:32, 40	488, 491

4:3	14:334; 15:400; 16:32	271, 474, 488
4:4	16:32, 250[c]	488, 574[c]
4:5	16:32	488
4:6	16:26, 32	486, 488
4:7	16:32	488
4:8	16:32	488
4:9	16:38	490
4:11	16:164–166, 178, 180	542–543, 548, 549
4:12	16:150, 164–166, 166, 178[c], 180[c]	536, 542–543, 543, 548[c], 549[c]
4:13	16:42, 138	491, 530
4:14	16:138	530
4:15	16:106, 114, 132, 144–146	518, 523, 528, 533
4:16	15:400; 16:138[c]	474, 530[c]
4:18	15:394, 398, 406	472, 473, 476
4:19	15:394, 406[c]	472, 476[c]
4:20	15:394, 400	472, 473–474
4:21	15:394, 398	472, 473
4:25	15:316, 334	444, 450
5:1	16:48	494
5:2	16:70	504
5:4	17:58	659
5:5	16:10, 76, 118; 17:58	480, 505, 524, 659
5:6	15:328	448
5:7	15:328[c]	448[c]
5:8	14:270; 15:252; 17:256	246–247, 416, 742
5:9	15:330; 16:26, 72	449, 486, 504
5:10	14:206; 15:286, 316, 328, 330, 332; 16:72	218, 431, 444, 448, 449, 450, 504
5:11	14:238; 15:332	231, 450
5:12	15:182, 202	384, 393
5:13	15:216	399
5:14	15:216	399
5:15	15:182, 250	384, 415
5:16	15:182; 16:24	384, 485
5:17	15:182, 250; 16:24	384, 415, 485
5:18	15:182, 318; 16:28	384, 444–445, 487
5:19	15:182, 322; 16:26 (twice)	384, 446, 486 (twice)
5:20	15:250; 16:106	415, 518
6:3	14:390; 16:184	290, 550
6:4	15:332, 334; 16:4 [5:4]	450 (twice), 477
6:5	15:332, 334	450 (twice)
6:6	15:192, 368–370	388, 462
6:8	15:332	450
6:9	15:310	441

6:11	15:332, 370; 16:4	450, 462, 477
6:12	16:12 (twice)	480 (twice)
6:13	16:12 (twice)	480 (twice)
6:14	16:124, 142	526, 532
6:15	16:142	532
6:16	15:206, 210	395, 397
6:17	14:20[12]; 15:206, 354–356	128[13], 395, 457
6:18	16:154	537
6:21	15:204, 380	394, 467
6:22	16:10, 154	480, 537
6:23	15:202; 17:20–22	393, 645
7:3	16:124[14], 134[c]	526[15], 529[c]
7:4	16:124, 134[c]	526, 529[c]
7:5	15:202; 16:106, 134[c]	393, 518, 529[c]
7:6	16:124, 134[c], 154	526, 529[c], 537
7:7	16:106, 124, 134[c]	518, 526, 529[c]
7:8	15:72, 192; 16:106	332, 388–389, 518
7:9	16:106[c]	518[c]
7:12	16:106	518
7:13	16:106–108	518
7:14	15:194, 206, 212	389, 395, 397
7:17	15:192	389
7:18	15:210; 16:14	397, 481
7:20	15:192	389
7:21	15:192, 210	389, 397
7:22	15:368	462
7:23	15:192, 208	389, 396
7:24	15:192, 208; 16:108	389, 396, 519
7:25	14:238; 15:212; 16:108[c]	231, 397, 519[c]
8:1	16:28	487
8:2	15:192; 16:134, 154	389, 529, 537
8:3	14:224; 15:206, 258–260, 304, 316	227, 395, 419, 438, 444
8:4	15:316; 16:142	444, 531
8:7	15:194, 206	389, 395
8:9	14:374; 16:58, 118[c]	287, 499, 524[c]
8:11	15:310–312, 368	442, 461–462
8:13	16:4	477
8:15	14:374; 15:204; 16:52, 72–74, 124–126, 138[c], 154	287, 394, 496, 505, 526, 530[c], 537
8:16	14:370, 374; 15:368; 16:52, 72[c], 74	286, 287, 461–462, 496, 505 (twice)[16]
8:17	15:332; 16:54	450, 496
8:18	15:390; 16:318; 17:22	470, 606, 645
8:19	16:380	633
8:20	15:216; 16:380	399, 633

8:21	15:216; 16:380	399, 633
8:22[o]	16:380[c]	633[c]
8:23	16:52, 380[c]	496, 633[c]
8:24	15:406; 16:380[c]	476, 633[c]
8:25	15:406; 17:66	476, 663
8:26	14:370; 15:294; 17:82–84	286, 435, 670
8:27	15:294; 17:82[c]	435, 670[c]
8:28	14:92, 118, 120; 15:344, 350	169, 181 (twice), 454, 456
8:29	14:90, 96, 118, 190; 15:10, 332, 344[c], 350[c]; 16:66	168, 171, 181, 211, 303, 450, 454[c], 456[c], 502
8:30	14:90, 118, 120; 15:344[c], 350[c]; 16:24, 66, 68	168, 181 (twice)[17], 454[c], 456, 485, 502, 503
8:32	14:186; 16:58	208, 499
8:33	14:116; 16:26	180, 486
8:34	15:294, 318, 330–332; 16:26, 28	434, 445, 449, 486, 487
8:35	15:286; 16:76, 318	431, 506, 605
8:38	15:36, 394; 16:76–78	315, 472, 506
8:39	16:76–78	506
9	14:98, 144, 156	172, 191, 196, 199[18]
9:1	14:110[c]	178[c]
9:3	14:110[x]; 17:256	178[x], 742
9:4	16:220; 17:256[x]	564, 742[x]
9:5	14:260; 15:260, 278	242, 419, 427
9:6	14:156[c]	196[c]
9:7	14:156; 16:176	196, 547
9:8	14:156; 16:176	196, 547
9:11	14:96, 158[19]	171, 197[20]
9:12	14:158[21]	197[22]
9:13	14:160[23]	198
9:14	14:162[24]	198
9:15	14:162[25]	198
9:16	14:132, 162[26]	187, 198
9:17	14:162[27]; 15:82	198, 337
9:18	14:104, 162; 15:70	176, 198, 331
9:19	14:164	199
9:20	14:146, 164	193, 199
9:21	14:146, 164 (twice)	193, 199 (twice)
9:22	14:96, 164[28]	171, 199
9:23	14:92, 102	169, 175
9:24	14:92	169
9:30	14:166; 16:32[c]	199, 488[c]
9:31	14:166; 15:212; 16:32	199, 397, 488
9:32	14:166; 16:32	199, 488
9:33	16:32[c]	488[c]

10:2	15:212; 17:154	397, 698
10:4	16:26, 108	486, 519
10:9	14:236, 354; 15:306, 402	231, 280, 439–440, 474
10:10	17:162	701
10:14	14:30; 15:346, 404; 16:122, 234; 17:82	133, 454, 475, 525, 568, 669
10:15	16:234	569
10:17	15:360	459
10:18	15:352; 16:122	457, 525
10:20	14:150	193
10:21	14:150	193
11	14:98	172
11:2	14:122	183
11:5	14:96	171
11:6	16:132	528
11:7	14:118, 146	180, 192
11:11	14:146; 15:80	192, 335
11:12	16:344	618
11:13	16:344[c]	618[c]
11:14	17:12	641
11:15	16:344	618
11:20	14:118, 122; 16:82	180, 183, 508
11:22	14:58, 118; 16:82	151, 180, 508
11:23	14:146	192
11:25	16:344	618
11:29	16:68, 82	503, 508
11:32	14:146	192
11:35	14:40[c]; 17:22	140[c], 645
11:36	14:40, 204, 322; 15:4–6, 20	140, 217, 267, 300, 307
12:[o,29]	16:320	607
12:1	16:154	537
12:2	15:342, 370; 16:12, 18, 154–156; 17:28	453, 462, 480, 482, 537, 648
12:3	17:34	650
12:4	16:58–60	499
12:5	16:58–60	499
12:7	16:238[c], 288	570[c], 594
12:8	16:238[c], 288	570[c], 594
12:9	17:204	720
12:10	17:236	733
12:11	17:152	697
12:13	17:382	792
12:14	17:102, 256[c]	677, 742[c]
12:15	17:266, 268	746, 747
12:17	17:12, 256	641, 742

12:18 17:282, 284 754 (twice)
12:19 17:284[c], 288 754[c], 755
12:20 17:256[c] 742[c]
12:21 17:256 742
13:1 16:332; 17:388, 398 611–612, 795, 799
13:3 17:388 795
13:4[30] 17:388 (twice) 795 (twice)
13:7 17:198, 364 718, 786
13:8 16:144 532–533
13:10 16:144 532–533
13:13 17:214, 218 725, 727
14 16:156 539
14:1 16:328 610
14:4 16:156, 266; 17:396 538, 584, 798
14:5 16:158; 17:178 539, 708
14:6[o] 17:178[q] 708–709[q]
14:8 16:156 538
14:9 15:310 441
14:10 15:12; 16:156, 354 304, 538–539, 622
14:11 15:12 304
14:12 16:356 623
14:13 16:162 541
14:14 17:112 681
14:15 17:282 753
14:17 15:298; 16:74; 17:112 436, 505, 681
14:19 17:270 748
14:20 16:126, 158 526, 539
14:21 16:158[c]; 17:14 539[c], 642 [16:21]
14:23 16:150[x], 158; 17:6 536[x], 539, 639
15[31] 16:156 539
15:4 16:252; 17:66 576, 663
15:5 14:234[c] 230[c]
15:6 14:234[c], 238 230[c], 231–232
15:7 16:66 502
15:8 15:304 439
15:13 14:372; 15:406 286, 476
15:27 16:298 597
16:2 17:382 792
16:5 16:308 602
16:17 14:12; 16:330 123, 610
16:18 14:12 123
16:19 17:28 648
16:20 15:300; 16:98 437, 515
16:25 14:234 (twice); 15:352 230 (twice), 456
16:26 14:44, 234 (twice) 143, 230 (twice)

16:27	14:56[c], 234 (twice)	150[c], 230 (twice)

1 Corinthians

1:1	14:226[c]	227[c]
1:2	14:226[c], 332; 16:232, 234	227[c], 271, 568 (twice)
1:3	14:226[c]	227[c]
1:4	14:238	232
1:7	14:284	252
1:8	14:284[c]; 16:68	252[c], 503
1:9	14:58; 15:6–8, 344, 344–346, 400; 16:58	151, 301–302, 454 (twice), 474, 499
1:11	17:328	772
1:13	14:390[c]	294[c]
1:14	14:390[c]	294[c]
1:15	14:390[c]	294[c]
1:17	16:206[c], 246	558[c], 573
1:18	16:260	580–581
1:19	17:36	650
1:21	14:26	130
1:23[o]	17:36[x]	650[x]
1:24	15:288; 17:36[x]	432, 650[x]
1:26	15:350	456
1:30	14:326; 16:2, 26; 17:28	269, 477, 486, 648
2:1	16:234	569
2:4	15:398; 16:234–236	473, 569
2:5	15:398	473
2:6	17:30	648
2:7	14:62, 64, 90, 102; 15:2; 17:32[c]	154 (twice), 168, 175, 299, 649[c]
2:8	15:306; 17:32	440, 649
2:9	16:374	631
2:10	14:384; 16:8	291, 478
2:11	14:384	291
2:12	16:8, 274	479, 587
2:13	16:118, 236	524, 569
2:14	15:206; 16:8[x], 260	395, 478–479[x], 581
2:15	16:8[x], 274, 304	479[x], 588, 601
2:16	16:274	588
3:3	17:274	749
3:7	16:236	569
3:8	16:244	572
3:9	16:234, 244–246[q]	568, 572[q]
3:11	16:230[c]	567[c]
3:13	15:338	452
3:15	15:338	452

3:16	14:382	290
3:19	17:36	650
3:22	15:402; 16:2	474, 477
3:23	14:350; 15:402; 16:2	278, 474, 477
4:1	14:18; 16:206, 238–240	127, 558, 570
4:2[o,1]	16:206	558
4:4	17:40	652
4:5	16:356	623
4:6	17:72	665
4:21	16:330	610
5:1	15:212	397
5:4	16:226–228, 326–328	566, 609
5:5	15:228; 16:332	404, 611
5:7	16:168	543
5:9	17:280	752
5:10	17:280	752
5:11	16:330, 334; 17:280	610, 612, 752
5:12	16:334	612
5:13	16:334[c]	612[c]
6:2	16:354 (twice)	622 (twice)
6:3	15:106; 16:354 (twice)[2]	348, 622 (twice)[3]
6:4	16:334; 17:36	612, 650
6:6	15:168	377
6:7	16:300[c]; 17:252, 314	598[c], 740, 767
6:9	16:28–30; 17:198, 218–220	487, 718, 727
6:10	16:28–30[c]; 17:214, 218–220	487[c], 725, 727
6:11	14:374, 392; 15:374; 16:26, 28–30, 184	287, 294–295, 464, 486, 487, 550
6:12	16:126	526
6:13	17:112, 220	681, 727
6:14	14:236; 16:350[c]	231, 620[c]
6:15	15:372[c]; 17:218	463[c], 727
6:16	15:126; 17:218	358, 727
6:17	16:56	498
6:18	17:218	727
6:19	14:382 (twice); 15:372	290, 291, 463
6:20	15:254, 316; 17:58	417, 444, 660
7	17:18	643
7:2	15:136, 154	362, 370
7:3	15:136; 17:348	362–363, 781
7:4	15:136	362
7:5	17:106	678
7:7	17:112[c]	681[c]
7:9[o]	17:112[x]	681[x]
7:12	15:154; 16:142, 272	369, 532, 586

7:14	17:160	700–701
7:15	15:174; 16:48, 272	379, 494, 587
7:20[o]	17:368 [7:21]	787 [7:21]
7:21	17:368 [7:22]	787 [7:22]
7:23	15:254; 16:154, 334	417, 537, 612
7:25	16:272	586
7:26	16:272; 17:112–114	586, 681
7:31	16:368; 17:52	628, 657
7:36	15:210; 16:272; 17:114 [36:37]	396, 587, 681
7:37	15:210; 17:114[c]	396, 681[c]
7:38	17:20	644
7:39	15:152, 210	369, 396
7:40	16:272	586–587
8:2	17:32	649
8:4	14:52, 202, 252, 378; 17:136	148, 216, 238, 288, 691
8:5	14:196, 202	213, 216
8:6	14:52, 182, 196, 202 (twice), 322; 15:6 (twice), 20	148, 206, 213, 216 (twice), 267, 300, 301, 307
8:7	17:42	653
8:8	17:112	681
8:9	16:158	540
8:10	17:142–144	694
8:13	16:158	539
9:5	15:154	370–371
9:7	16:292[4]; 17:20[c], 410	595[5], 644[c], 804
9:9	15:62	329
9:11	16:298[c]	597[c]
9:14	16:292	595
9:15	16:294	596
9:17	15:212	397
9:18	16:294; 17:20[c]	596, 644[c]
9:19	16:158, 162	540, 541
9:20	16:158	540
9:21	16:158	540
9:22	16:158	540
9:27	14:118; 16:84; 17:202	180, 509, 720
10:2	14:390; 16:174, 190	294, 546, 552
10:3	16:174, 196	546, 554
10:4	16:174, 196, 200, 230[c]	546, 554, 555, 567[c]
10:6	17:136[c], 204	691[c], 720
10:7	17:136	691
10:9	14:286, 290, 360	254, 255, 282
10:11	16:252	576
10:12	16:80	507
10:13	14:58; 15:88, 400	151, 339, 474

10:14	17:136[c], 144	691[c], 694
10:15	16:254, 304	577, 601
10:16	16:196, 206[c]	554, 558[c]
10:17	16:196, 206[c]	554, 558[c]
10:20	17:144	694
10:21	16:196[c]	554[c]
10:22	17:148	696
10:23[o]	16:126, 158	526, 540
10:31	17:10, 160	640, 700
10:32	17:12	641–642
10:33	17:12–14	641–642
11:3	14:204, 350; 17:350 (twice)[6]	217, 278, 782 (twice)[7]
11:4	16:144; 17:90	533, 673
11:7	15:120; 17:350[x]	355, 782[x]
11:8	15:120; 17:350[x]	355, 782[x]
11:9	15:120	355
11:10	15:102; 17:220	346, 727
11:17	16:320	607
11:18	16:320	607
11:19	15:66, 80; 16:312	330, 335, 604
11:20	16:194	554
11:23	16:194–196	554
11:24[o]	16:194–196	554
11:25	16:112, 194–196, 200[c]	522, 554, 555[c]
11:26[o]	16:194–196	554
11:27[o]	16:194–196[c]	554[c]
11:28	16:194–196[c], 208	554[c], 559
11:29	16:194–196[c], 210	554[c], 559
11:30	16:194–196[c], 210[q]	554[c], 559[q]
11:31	17:62	661
11:32	15:388	469
12:3	14:372; 15:394; 16:118[c]	286, 471, 524[c]
12:4	14:394	295
12:5	14:394	295
12:6	14:394	295
12:8	16:266[c]	584[c]
12:9	15:364; 16:266[c]	460, 584[c]
12:10	16:274	588
12:11	14:388	293
12:12	16:60	499
12:13	14:390; 15:368; 16:60, 184, 188[c]	294, 462, 499, 550, 552[c]
12:27	16:60	499
12:28	16:236, 238[c], 288	569 (twice)[8], 594
12:31	16:226	566
13	16:10; 17:196	479, 717

13:1	16:226; 17:198	566, 718
13:2	15:364	460
13:3	17:378	791
13:5	17:310	765
13:6	17:310	765
13:7[o]	17:310[x]	765[x]
13:8	16:222, 226	564, 566
13:9	16:8	479
13:12	14:30; 15:30–32; 16:374–376	133, 312, 631
13:13	16:10, 226	479, 566
14	16:260	580
14:1	16:244, 262	572, 582
14:3	16:244	572
14:15[9]	17:88 (twice)	672 (twice)
14:16[10]	17:88 (twice)	672 (twice)
14:20	17:316	767
14:22	16:222	564
14:26	16:324	608
14:34	16:326	609
14:35	16:326	609
14:40	16:320	607
15	15:248	414
15:3	15:316	444
15:4	15:306, 312	439, 442
15:10	17:4	638
15:13	15:334; 16:350	450, 620
15:17	15:224, 332	402, 449
15:18	15:224	402
15:19	15:224; 16:352	402–403, 620
15:20	15:334; 16:350	450, 620[c]
15:21	15:216, 276	399, 426
15:22	15:182	384
15:23	16:350, 362	620, 625
15:24	15:302; 16:360, 362, 366	437, 624, 625, 626
15:25	16:362[c], 366	625[c], 626
15:26	15:300; 16:362[c], 366	437, 625[c], 626
15:27	14:204, 262, 352; 16:366	217, 243, 278, 626
15:28	14:204, 352[q]; 15:302; 16:366	217, 278[q], 437, 626
15:29	15:224	403
15:30	15:224; 16:352	403, 620
15:31	16:352[c]; 17:130[11]	620[c], 689[12]
15:32	15:224; 16:352[c]	403, 620[c]
15:33	17:278	751
15:41	16:378	632
15:42	15:224; 16:376, 378	403, 631, 632

15:43	15:224; 16:376	403, 631
15:44	15:44, 224, 240; 16:376[q]	320, 403, 408, 631[q]
15:45	15:40, 224	318, 403
15:46	15:44, 224	320, 403
15:47	15:224, 260	403, 419
15:48	15:224	403
15:49	15:44, 224	320, 403
15:50	15:224	403
15:51	16:352	621
15:52	15:230; 16:350, 352[c]	405, 620, 621[c]
15:53	16:352	621
15:54	16:348[c]	619[c]
15:56	15:300 [15:54, 57]	437 [15:54, 57]
15:57	15:300 [15:54, 57]	437 [15:54, 57]
16:2	17:188	713
16:19	16:308[c]	602[c]
16:22	16:332	611

2 Corinthians

1:1	14:226[c]; 16:234	227[c], 568
1:2	14:226[c]	227[c]
1:3	14:58, 226[c], 238	150, 227[c], 232
1:4	15:392	470
1:8	15:388	470
1:9	15:388	470
1:10	15:388	470
1:12	17:40–42, 316	653, 767
1:21	14:234, 374; 16:68	230–231, 287, 503
1:22	14:234, 374, 378; 16:68	230–231, 287, 289, 503
1:23	17:118	684
1:24	16:82, 310; 17:396	508, 603, 798
2:6	16:330	610
2:7	16:328, 332	609, 611
2:8	16:328, 332[c]	609, 611[c]
2:16	15:332	450
2:17	17:414–416	805
3:3	16:118, 126, 142[1], 148[2], 270	524, 526, 532[3], 534[4],586
3:4	15:396, 402	472, 474
3:5	14:136; 15:206; 17:4	188, 395, 638
3:6	16:110, 112, 118, 126	519, 522, 524, 526
3:7	16:126, 134[5]	526, 529[6]
3:8	16:126	526
3:11	16:114, 118–120, 126	522, 524, 526
3:12[o]	16:114[q]	522[q]

3:13	16:114[q], 126	522[q], 526
3:14	16:112[7]	522[8]
3:17	16:152	536
3:18	15:52	324
4:2	16:260–262	581
4:3	16:260–262	581
4:4	14:350 [4:46]; 15:84, 108, 206	278, 337, 348, 395
4:5	16:234	568
4:6	14:326, 350; 15:6, 16, 354	269, 278, 300, 306, 457
4:8	16:318[c]	605[c]
4:9	16:318	605–606
4:10	16:4	477
4:13	15:394; 17:162	471, 701
4:14	14:330; 16:350	270, 620
4:16	15:342; 16:16, 376[c]	453, 482, 631[c]
4:17	15:336, 390; 16:376	451, 470, 631
4:18	15:398	473
5:1[9]	15:246 (twice), 340; 16:376	413 (twice), 452, 631
5:2[o]	15:246	413
5:3	15:246 (twice)	413 (twice)
5:4	15:246 (twice); 16:352	413 (twice), 621
5:5	15:246 (twice)	413 (twice)
5:6	15:246, 248	413, 413–414
5:7	15:246, 248, 398	413, 414, 473
5:8	15:246, 248 (twice)	413 (twice), 414
5:9	15:246, 248 (twice)	413 (twice), 414
5:10	15:246, 248, 340; 16:352, 354, 356	413, 414, 452, 621, 622, 623
5:14[o]	15:318 [5:15]	445 [5:15]
5:16	17:136	691
5:17	14:326; 15:370, 372; 16:126	269, 462, 463, 526
5:18	14:264, 326; 15:286; 16:114	244, 269, 431, 523
5:19	14:264, 300, 326; 15:286, 332; 16:26[c], 114	244, 259, 269, 431, 450, 486[c], 523
5:20	14:326; 15:344	269, 454
5:21	14:326; 15:292, 316, 318–320, 330; 16:26	269, 433, 444, 445, 449, 486
6:1	14:116, 150[c]; 16:12	180, 193[c], 480
6:2	14:150; 15:360	193, 458
6:3	17:46[c]	655[c]
6:4[o,10]	17:46	655
6:8	17:240	735
6:14	15:152–154; 17:404–406	369, 802
6:16	14:382; 16:60; 17:144	290, 499, 694
6:18[11]	14:48	145
7:1	16:12; 17:10	480, 641

7:8	17:328	772
7:10	15:358, 364, 380	458, 460, 467
7:11	15:380	467
8:1	16:308	602
8:3	17:374, 378	789–790, 791
8:8	17:378	791
8:9	15:304; 17:242	439, 736
8:11	17:46	655
8:12	17:44, 374	654, 789
8:13	17:374 (twice)[12]	789[c], 790
8:16	17:266	746
8:19	16:310	603
8:24	17:12, 378	641, 791
9:6	17:380 (twice)	792 (twice)
9:7	17:44 (twice)	654 (twice)
9:8	17:378	791
9:9	17:378	791
10:3	16:334	612
10:4	15:298; 16:334, 336	436, 612, 613
10:5[o]	16:336[x]	613[x]
10:6[o]	16:336[x]	613[x]
10:13	17:236	733
10:15	16:16; 17:236	481, 733
11:3	17:316	767
11:5	16:228	566–567
11:8	16:294, 296	596, 597
11:9	16:294, 296	596, 597
11:10	16:294	596
11:12	16:294; 17:20[c]	596, 644[c]
11:13	16:292	595
11:14	15:34	315
11:15	15:34	315
11:23	17:20	644
11:26	17:274	750
11:32	16:316	605
11:33	16:316[c]	605[c]
12:2	15:30	312
12:4	15:30	312
12:8	17:102	676
12:9	17:102	676
12:10	17:66	663
12:14	16:294	596
12:17	16:294	596
12:18	16:294	596
12:19	16:294	597

13:3	15:290; 16:248	433, 574
13:4	15:312	442
13:5	16:70	504
13:10	16:332	611
13:11	16:18; 17:270	482, 748
13:14[o,13]	14:392; 16:58, 118	295, 499, 524

Galatians

1:1	14:224, 236; 15:306; 16:240	227, 231, 440, 570
1:2	16:308	602
1:4	14:238; 15:284, 316	232, 431, 444
1:5	14:238	232
1:6	15:346	454
1:8	16:224, 282	564, 591
1:11	14:18	127
1:12	14:18	127
1:17	16:240	570
1:22	16:308	602
1:23	14:24	129
2:4	16:160; 17:274	540, 750
2:5	16:160	540
2:6	16:240	570
2:8	16:228[c]	566[c]
2:9	16:228 (twice)[c]	566 (twice)[c]
2:11	16:162, 228[c]	541, 566[c]
2:16	16:32, 36[c]	488, 489[c]
2:19	16:4	477
2:20	15:332, 402; 16:4	450, 474, 477
2:21	16:32–34	488
3:8	16:34	488
3:9	16:34	488
3:10	16:34, 106, 132[c], 140	488, 518, 529[c], 531
3:11	16:34, 108, 136[c]	488, 519, 529[c]
3:12	16:34, 106, 132[c]	488, 518, 529[c]
3:13	15:254–256, 292, 304; 16:108, 132[1], 140[2]	417, 433, 439, 519, 529[3], 531[4]
3:18	16:138 (twice)	530 (twice)
3:19	14:278; 15:286[5]; 16:108, 126	251, 431[6], 518–519, 526
3:20	14:52, 206	148, 218
3:21	16:108	519
3:22	15:402; 16:108–110	474, 519
3:24	14:18; 16:110	126, 519
3:25	16:126	526–527
3:26	15:402; 16:50	474, 495

3:27[o]	16:184	550
3:29[o]	16:54	496
4:1	16:126, 138	527, 530
4:2[o]	16:126[q]	527[q]
4:3[o]	16:126[q]	527[q]
4:4	15:254, 258, 260; 16:52, 126–128[q], 150[c]	417, 418, 419, 495, 527[q], 535[c]
4:5	15:316; 16:52, 126–128[q], 150	443, 495, 527[q], 535
4:6	14:374, 378; 15:296, 368; 16:52	287, 289, 435, 462, 495
4:7	16:54, 154	496, 537
4:8	14:38; 17:50, 74[7]	137, 656, 666[8]
4:9	17:176	708
4:10	17:176	708
4:21	16:128[c], 138[c]	527[c], 530[c]
4:24	16:112, 128, 138[c]	522, 527, 530[c]
4:26	16:60, 128, 138[c], 284	499, 527, 530[c], 592
4:29	16:316	605
4:30	16:128, 138[c]	527, 530[c]
5:1	16:154	537
5:3	15:304; 16:166, 178[c]	439, 543, 548[c]
5:4	16:96, 138 (twice)	513, 530 (twice)
5:5	15:406	476
5:6	16:10, 38; 17:196	479, 490, 718
5:12	17:98	676
5:13	16:158	540
5:14	16:144	533
5:16	16:12, 18; 17:202[c]	480, 482, 720[c]
5:17	15:194; 16:14; 17:202	389, 481, 720
5:18	16:128, 138	527, 530–531
5:19	17:136	691
5:20	17:136, 274	691, 749
5:21	17:136[x], 214, 274	691[x], 725, 749
5:22	15:394; 16:10, 134[c]; 17:4, 196	471, 480, 529[c], 639, 717
5:23	16:134[c]	529[c]
5:24	17:202	720
5:26	17:238	734
6:1	16:328; 17:272	610, 749
6:2	17:272	749
6:6	16:292	595
6:8	17:10	641
6:9	17:44	654
6:10	17:254, 344	741, 779
6:12	17:74	667
6:14	16:18	482
6:15	15:372	463

Ephesians

1:3	14:238; 15:342; 16:2–4, 66	232, 453, 477, 502
1:4	14:96, 100 (twice)[1], 104; 16:8, 46	171, 173 (twice)[2], 175,479, 493
1:5	14:90, 100, 104, 104–106; 15:342; 16:50	168, 173, 175, 176, 453, 495
1:6	14:102; 15:332	175, 450
1:9	14:62, 88; 15:250, 262	153, 167, 415, 420
1:10	14:88; 15:98, 250–252, 254, 262, 318	167, 344, 415, 417, 420, 445
1:11	14:62, 64[c], 90, 100, 104, 106; 15:54	153, 154[c], 169, 173, 175, 176, 326
1:12	15:400	474
1:13	14:116, 370[3], 374; 16:74	180, 286[4], 287, 505
1:14	14:370[5], 374; 16:74	286[6], 287, 505
1:17	14:204, 350–352; 15:354	217, 278, 457
1:18	15:354	457
1:19	15:312	442
1:20	14:306; 15:296, 312, 314	261, 435, 442 (twice)
1:21	14:306; 15:36, 296	261, 315, 435
1:22	15:296, 298; 16:60	435, 436, 499
1:23	16:60	499
2:1	15:204	394
2:2	15:84, 108, 110, 206	337, 348, 349, 395
2:3	15:194–196, 342	389, 453
2:4	14:58, 104; 15:368, 376[c]	150, 175, 462, 464[c]
2:5	14:104; 15:334, 342, 368, 376	175, 450, 453, 462, 464
2:6	15:334; 16:376	450, 631
2:8	15:392; 16:34, 40	471, 488, 491
2:9	16:34, 40	488–489, 491
2:10	15:372; 16:40; 17:6	463, 491, 639
2:12	16:104, 128, 220	518, 527, 564
2:14	16:104[c], 128	517–518[c], 527
2:15	16:128	527
2:16	16:128	527
2:18	14:238, 374; 15:406	232, 287, 475
2:19	16:54, 62	497, 500
2:20	16:62[7], 228, 230[c], 252, 268	500[8], 567 (twice)[9], 576, 585–586
2:21[o,10]	16:62	500
2:22	14:384; 16:62–64[11]	291, 500[12]
3:4	15:262	420
3:5	15:352	456
3:8	17:236	733
3:9	14:182; 15:6, 262	206, 301, 420
3:10	14:64, 104; 15:36, 98, 106	154, 175, 315, 344, 348

3:11	14:64, 92, 104; 15:396	154, 169, 175, 472–473
3:12	15:396, 406	472–473, 475
3:14	14:238	232
3:16	16:68	503
3:17	16:10, 58, 66[q], 70, 82 [3:18]	480, 499, 502[q], 504, 508 [3:18]
3:18	15:286[c]; 16:22, 66	431[c], 484, 502
3:19	14:338; 15:286; 16:22, 66	273, 431, 484, 502
3:20	14:238	232
3:21	14:238	232
4:1	16:320	607
4:2	16:320; 17:208, 272	607, 722, 749
4:3	16:320; 17:254	607, 741–742
4:4	14:206	217
4:5	14:206, 276[c]	217, 250[c]
4:6	14:46, 52, 206	144, 148, 217
4:8	14:276[c], 328; 15:298, 312	250[c], 269, 436, 442
4:9	14:276	250
4:10	15:28, 312	311, 442
4:11	16:238, 266[c]	569–570, 584[c]
4:12	16:238, 266[c]	569–570, 584[c]
4:13	16:60, 120, 238, 266[c]	499–500, 524, 569–570, 584[c]
4:14	16:304	601
4:15	16:16, 60; 17:270	482, 499–500, 748–749
4:16	16:60–62	499–500
4:17	17:30[c]	649[c]
4:18	15:204, 206; 17:30	394, 395, 649
4:20	16:12[c]	480[c]
4:21	16:12	480
4:22	15:192, 194; 16:12	388, 389, 480
4:23	15:342, 370; 16:12	453, 462, 480
4:24	14:364; 15:52, 342, 370, 372; 16:12	284, 324, 453, 462, 463, 480
4:25	17:296	759
4:26	17:208	722
4:28	17:114, 330, 372	681, 773, 789
4:29	17:322	770
4:30	14:370, 374, 378; 16:74	286, 287, 288, 505
4:31	17:208	722
5:1	17:270[c]	748[c]
5:2	15:256 (twice), 292, 330	417 (twice), 434, 449
5:3	17:220	727
5:4	17:220, 222, 320, 322–324	727, 728, 769, 770
5:5	17:220, 230	727, 731
5:6	14:164	199
5:7	17:278	751

5:8	15:206	395
5:9	17:6	639
5:11	17:278	751
5:15	17:28	648
5:17	17:30–32	649
5:18	17:216	725
5:19	17:118	683
5:20	17:118 (twice)	683 (twice)
5:21	17:236	733
5:22	17:350	782
5:23	15:320; 16:62; 17:350	446, 500, 782
5:24	17:350	782
5:25	15:320, 374, 376; 17:350	446, 464 (twice), 782
5:26	15:368, 374; 16:168, 184, 198, 202	462, 464, 544, 550, 555, 557
5:27	16:30	487
5:29[13]	17:200 (twice)	719 (twice)
6:1	17:356	784
6:2	17:356	784
6:3	17:356[c]	784[c]
6:4	17:354	783
6:5	17:370	788
6:6	17:70, 370[c]	664, 788[c]
6:7	17:70, 370[c]	664, 788[c]
6:8	17:370[c]	788[c]
6:9	17:366	787
6:10	16:20	483
6:11[o,14]	16:20	483
6:12	15:108, 110	348, 349
6:14	16:304	601
6:17	16:270	586
6:18	17:84, 94, 96	670, 674, 674–675
6:19	17:96	674–675
6:20	17:326	771

Philippians

1:1	16:286	593
1:2	14:238, 266–268[c]	232, 245[c]
1:3	14:238–240; 16:16	232, 481
1:6	16:16	481
1:8	17:118[c]	684[c]
1:9	17:36	651
1:10	17:36	651
1:11	17:2, 10	637, 640
1:12	15:80	336

1:14	15:80; 17:164	336, 702
1:15	17:78	668
1:16	16:312; 17:78[c]	603, 668[c]
1:20	17:162	701
1:23	15:240	408–409
1:29	15:392; 17:162	471, 701–702
2:2	17:270	749
2:3	17:236	733
2:6	14:272–274, 342, 350; 15:292, 302, 306	248–249[1], 274–275, 278, 434, 438, 440
2:7	14:306[c,2]; 15:260, 292, 302, 306	261[c,3], 419, 434, 438, 440
2:8	15:256, 260, 302, 304, 306–308	417, 419, 438, 439, 440
2:9	14:306, 330; 15:12, 310, 312	261, 271, 304, 441, 442
2:10	14:330; 15:12, 98	271, 304, 344
2:11	14:330; 15:12	271, 304
2:12	15:356; 16:80; 17:60, 200	457, 507, 660, 719
2:13	14:136; 15:356, 370; 17:6	188[4], 457, 462, 639
2:15	16:52; 17:40	496, 652
2:16	15:224–226	403
2:17	16:318	606
3:1	16:252	576
3:2	16:304	601
3:6	15:212	397
3:7	17:52[c]	657[c]
3:8	17:52	657
3:9	16:34, 42	488, 492
3:10	15:332–334	450
3:11	15:226	403
3:12	14:118; 16:16	180, 482
3:14	15:336; 17:10	451, 641
3:15	16:22, 254, 266	483, 577, 584
3:16	16:266	584
3:17	17:420	807
3:18	17:420[c]	807[c]
3:19	15:206	395
3:20	15:226; 16:378	403, 632
3:21	14:318; 15:226, 334; 16:376	266, 403, 450, 631
4:3	14:92	170[5]
4:5	17:310	765
4:6	14:354; 17:80	280, 669
4:7	14:354–356; 16:48	280, 494
4:8	17:2, 26	637, 647
4:9[o]	17:2–4[x]	637[x]
4:11	17:224	729
4:12	17:224	729

4:15	16:296	597
4:16[o]	16:296[x]	597[x]
4:17[o]	16:296[x]	597[x]
4:18[o]	16:296[x]	597[x]
4:21[o]	16:14	481
4:22	16:14[c]	481[c]

Colossians

1:3	14:240[c]	232[c]
1:11	17:66, 208	663, 722
1:12	15:338	451
1:13	15:56, 206	327, 395
1:15	14:182, 190, 306–308, 350; 15:8–10[1], 10	206, 211, 261, 278, 302–303[2], 303
1:16	14:182, 306–308; 15:6, 10, 28, 32, 36	206, 261, 301, 303, 311, 313, 315
1:17	14:306–308, 324; 15:56	261, 268, 327
1:18	14:182 (twice)[c], 190; 15:8–10[3], 298, 334; 16:61	206[c], 207[c], 211, 302–303[4], 436, 450, 500
1:19	14:338; 15:56; 16:62[c]	273, 327, 500[c]
1:20	15:98, 292, 318	344, 434, 445
1:22	15:292	434
1:24	15:334; 16:62	450, 500
1:26	15:262[c], 352	420[c], 457
1:27	15:262	420
1:28	16:18	482
2:1	17:270[c]	749[c]
2:2	14:224, 264, 354; 15:262; 16:22; 17:270	227, 244, 280, 420, 483–484, 749
2:3	15:262; 17:28	420, 648
2:5	16:64, 320–322	500, 607
2:8	14:20; 16:282; 17:36	127, 591, 650
2:9	14:38[5], 338; 15:24, 260	137[6], 273, 310, 419
2:11	16:166, 176	543, 547
2:12	15:312; 16:184, 198	442, 550, 555
2:13	15:204	394
2:14	15:310, 316; 16:28, 110, 128	441, 443–444, 487, 519, 527
2:15	15:110, 310; 16:128[c]	349, 441, 527[c]
2:16	16:128[c]; 17:174, 176, 192	527[c], 707, 708, 714
2:17	14:18; 16:128[c]; 17:174, 176[c]	127, 527[c], 707, 708[c]
2:18	15:36; 17:144, 396	315, 694, 798
2:19	16:62	500
2:20	17:112	681
2:21[o]	17:112[q]	681[q]

2:22[o]	17:112[q]	681[q]
2:23	17:64–66	662
3:1	15:334	450
3:2	15:334	450
3:3	14:224; 16:4	227, 477
3:5	16:12; 17:202, 230	480, 720, 731
3:8	17:314, 324	766, 770
3:9	15:192, 370 (twice), 372; 16:12	388, 462 (twice), 463, 480
3:10	15:52, 342, 370 (twice), 372; 16:12	324, 453, 462 (twice), 463, 480
3:11	15:370 (twice), 372	462 (twice), 463
3:12	14:96; 17:272	171, 749
3:13	17:272	749
3:14[o]	17:272[c]	749[c]
3:15	16:48; 17:270–272	494, 749
3:16	16:6, 320; 17:118	478, 607, 683
3:17	14:240, 332	232, 271
3:18	17:350	782
3:19	17:350	782
3:20	17:356	784
3:21	17:354	783
3:22	17:370[c]	788[c]
3:23	17:40, 192–194	652, 716
4:1	17:366	787
4:2	17:86, 216	671, 726
4:3	15:262; 17:96	420, 675
4:6	17:322	770
4:12	16:18; 17:94	482, 674
4:15	16:308	602
4:16	16:270	586

1 Thessalonians

1:1	16:60	499
1:2	14:240	232
1:3	14:240	232
1:5	15:394	472
1:9	14:40, 236[c], 240; 17:144	140, 231[c], 232, 694
1:10	14:236, 240	231, 232
2:5	17:316, 416	767, 805
2:6	17:238	734
2:12	15:346; 16:66	454, 502
2:13	15:398	473
2:14	16:308[c]	602[c]
2:18	15:110	349
3:3	15:392	470

3:11	14:224	227
3:12	14:284	252
3:13	14:284	252
4:3	17:216–218	726
4:4	17:202	720
4:5	17:202[c]	720[c]
4:6	17:332	774
4:7	15:374	464
4:8	14:380; 16:118	290, 524
4:9	14:18; 16:6; 17:272	127, 478, 749
4:11	17:232	732
4:12	17:232	732
4:13	15:230–232; 17:262	405–406, 744
4:14	14:330; 15:230–232, 334; 16:350[c]	270, 405–406, 450, 620[c]
4:15	15:230–232; 16:352	405–406, 621
4:16	15:36, 106, 230–232; 16:346, 352 [4:17]	315, 347, 405–406, 618, 621 [4:17]
4:17	15:230–232; 16:352 [4:18], 376	405–406, 621 [4:18], 631
4:18	16:320	607
5:2	16:340	615
5:3	16:340	615
5:6	17:216	726
5:8	17:212	724
5:9	14:92; 15:286	169, 431
5:10	15:286[c]	431[c]
5:12	17:420	807
5:13	17:420	807
5:14	16:328, 330; 17:252	610 (twice), 740
5:15	17:256, 344	742, 779
5:17	17:94	674
5:19[o]	14:370; 16:74	286, 505
5:21[o]	16:304	601
5:23[o]	15:40–42, 246, 368, 372	318–319, 413, 462, 463
5:27[o]	16:252; 17:132	576, 689

2 Thessalonians

1:1	16:60[c]	499[c]
1:2	14:240[c]	232[c]
1:3	14:240[c]; 16:16	232[c], 481
1:5	15:336	451
1:6	15:336; 16:318	451, 606
1:7	15:34, 98, 336; 16:318, 338 (twice), 346	315, 344, 451, 606, 614, 615, 619
1:8	16:122, 338[c], 346	525, 615[c], 619

1:9	16:122[c], 370, 372	525[c], 628, 629
1:10	15:400; 16:346	474, 618
1:11	15:338, 394; 16:96	451, 471, 514
2:1	16:344	618
2:2	16:274, 344	587, 618
2:3	16:314, 342 (twice), 344	604, 617 (twice), 618
2:4[o]	16:314[q]	604[q]
2:8	14:272[c]; 15:14; 16:342, 364	248[c], 305, 617, 625
2:9	14:272[c]; 15:94; 16:224	248[c], 341, 564–565
2:10	14:172; 15:84[c], 328	202, 337[c], 448–449
2:11	14:172–174; 15:70, 84	202, 332, 337
2:12	14:156, 174	196, 202
2:13	14:96, 116; 15:344, 374, 404	171, 180, 454, 464, 475
2:14	15:344, 346; 16:66	454 (twice), 502
2:16	14:224	227
3:2	14:174	202
3:3[o]	16:94[q]	513[q]
3:5	17:66	663
3:6	14:128[c]; 16:330	185[c], 610
3:7	16:294	596
3:8	16:294	596
3:9	16:294	596
3:10	17:232, 264, 374	732, 746, 790
3:11	14:128; 17:374–376	185, 790
3:12	17:232, 374–376	732, 790
3:13	17:44	654
3:14	16:330	610
3:15	16:332	611
3:17	16:274	587

1 Timothy

1:1	15:254	416
1:4	16:282	591
1:5	16:144	533
1:9	16:134[c]	529[c]
1:10	17:334	774
1:11	14:60	151
1:13	17:32, 156	649, 699
1:15	15:286, 326; 17:64	431, 448, 662
1:17	14:44, 46, 56[c]	143, 144, 150[c]
1:19	14:22; 15:362; 16:86; 17:40, 156	129, 459, 509, 652, 699
1:20	16:332; 17:156	611, 699
2:1	15:326; 17:94, 96[c], 398	448, 674, 675[c], 799
2:2	17:94[c], 96, 398	674[c], 675, 799

2:3	15:254, 326[q]; 17:94[c]	416–417, 448[q], 674[c]
2:4	14:96, 150[c]; 15:318, 326[q]	171, 193[c], 445, 448[q]
2:5	14:52, 206; 15:256, 278	148, 217, 418, 427
2:6	15:256, 316[1], 318[c]	417, 444[2], 445[c]
2:8	17:82, 86, 92	669, 671, 673
2:9	17:222	728
2:11	16:326	609
2:12	15:120; 16:326	355, 609
2:13	15:120	355
2:14	15:120, 180	355, 382
3	15:144	365–366
3:1	16:286[c], 290[c]	593[c], 595[c]
3:2	15:136, 154; 16:286	362, 371, 594
3:3	16:300	598
3:4	15:154	371
3:5	16:286; 17:366	594, 787
3:8	16:300[c]	598[c]
3:10	16:288, 290	594, 595
3:13	16:288 (twice)	594 (twice)
3:14[o]	16:268[c]	585[c]
3:15	16:220, 252, 268, 278	563–564, 576, 585, 589
3:16	14:264, 266; 15:260, 262	244, 245, 419, 420
4:1	15:362; 16:96, 342[c]; 17:164	459, 513, 617[c], 702
4:2	17:42	653
4:3	17:112, 114	681 (twice)
4:4	15:14; 17:112, 160	305, 681, 700
4:5	17:160	700
4:6	16:236	569
4:8	17:114	681
4:10	15:62, 254	329, 417
4:12	17:12, 360	641, 785
4:14	16:214[c], 290	561[c], 595
5:1	16:330	610
5:3[3]	16:288	594
5:4	17:256, 356	742, 784
5:8	15:172; 17:348	379, 781
5:12	15:362	460
5:13	17:312	766
5:17	16:286–288, 292	594, 595 [5:7]
5:18	16:292[q]	595[q]
5:20	16:328–330	610
5:21	14:88, 98, 398; 15:98	167, 172, 297, 344
5:22	16:290	595
5:23	17:200	719
6:1	17:156, 370	699, 788

6:2	17:370	788
6:3	16:282	591
6:4	16:282[q]; 17:312	591[q], 765
6:6	17:224	729
6:7	17:224	729
6:8[o]	17:224[q]	729[q]
6:9	17:228	731
6:10	17:230	731
6:12	15:346; 16:18; 17:162	454, 482, 701
6:13	14:234 (twice); 17:162	230 (twice), 701
6:14	14:234 (twice), 330, 342; 17:162	230 (twice), 270, 274, 701
6:15	14:48[4], 60, 234 (twice)	145[5], 151, 230 (twice)
6:16	14:30, 234 (twice), 250; 15:28	133, 230 (twice), 237, 311
6:17	17:226	730
6:18	17:226[c], 380[c]	730[c], 792[c]
6:19	17:380	792

2 Timothy

1:3	14:240; 17:40	232, 652
1:6	16:214[c]	561[c]
1:7	17:250	739
1:9	14:44, 92, 100; 15:344, 350	144, 169, 173, 454, 456
1:12	15:394	472
1:13	14:20[1], 20–22[2], 22	128 (twice)[3], 129
1:14	14:18–20	127–128
1:16	17:162	701
2:2	16:242–244	572
2:3	15:392	470
2:10	14:118	180
2:11	15:332	450
2:12	14:118[c]; 15:332; 17:162	180[c], 450, 701
2:13	14:48, 58, 106, 118; 15:400	146, 151, 176, 180, 474
2:19	14:106, 122, 332; 16:76	176, 183, 271, 506
2:21	14:128, 164; 16:12–14	185, 199, 480–481
2:22	14:332	271
2:25	15:378	466
2:26	15:206	395
3:1	16:340[q]	616[q]
3:2	17:200	719
3:12	16:318	606
3:15	16:252, 258, 260[q]; 17:360	576, 578, 580[q], 785
3:16	16:248, 252–254	574, 576–577
3:17	16:252, 260[q]; 17:4	576, 580[q], 637
4:1	14:224	227

4:2	16:236	569
4:3	16:306	601
4:5	16:240	570
4:7	16:18; 17:40	482, 652
4:8	15:224, 336, 340; 16:376; 17:40[c]	403, 451, 452, 631, 652[c]
4:14	17:98	676
4:20	16:224	565

Titus

1:1	14:116; 16:8	180, 473, 479
1:2	14:44[c], 48, 100[c]; 15:400; 16:8	144[c], 146, 173[c], 473, 479
1:3	15:254	417
1:5	16:286, 290[c]	593, 595[c]
1:6	15:136, 144	362, 365–366
1:7	16:286, 288, 300[c]	593, 594, 598[c]
1:11	16:300[c]	598[c]
1:12	17:326	771
1:14	16:282	591
1:15	15:204; 16:126; 17:42	394, 526, 653
2:2	17:360	785
2:4	17:12, 350–352	641, 782
2:5	17:156[c], 350–352	699[c], 782
2:6	17:360	785
2:7	17:12, 416	641, 805
2:9	17:370	788
2:10	15:254; 17:370	417, 788
2:11	17:4, 212	637, 724
2:12	17:4, 212	637, 724
2:13	14:266, 268; 16:346	245, 246, 618
2:14	15:316, 320, 326–328, 330, 374	444, 445, 448, 449, 464
3:1	17:398–400	799
3:2	17:284	754
3:4	15:254	417
3:5	15:254, 342, 368 (twice); 16:42, 184, 202	417, 453, 462 (twice), 492, 550, 557
3:6	15:254; 16:42–44	417, 492
3:7	16:24, 42–44, 54	485, 492, 496
3:8	14:22, 334; 17:4	129, 272, 637
3:10	16:330	610

Philemon

	17:368[1]	787[2]
v. 2	16:308	602

v. 3	14:268[c]	245[c]
v. 4°	14:240[c,3]	232[c]
v. 5	14:240[c], 332	232[c], 271

Hebrews

1:1	14:280, 368	251, 285
1:2	14:182, 192, 350; 15:6, 56, 288 [1:1]	206, 211, 278, 301, 327, 432 [1:1]
1:3	14:40, 192, 324, 350; 15:56, 314, 330	140, 211, 268, 278, 327, 442, 449
1:4	14:184, 306, 350	207, 261, 278
1:5	14:88, 182–184, 184 (twice)	166, 207 (three times)
1:6	14:184, 190, 244[c], 330–332; 15:98	207, 211, 234[c], 271, 344
1:7	15:32, 34, 140	313, 314, 364
1:8	14:258, 314 [2:8], 348; 16:366	240, 264, 277, 626–627
1:9	14:258, 348	240–241, 277
1:10	14:182; 15:6	206, 301
1:11	14:314 [2:11]	264
1:12	14:314 [2:12]	264
1:14	15:34, 100; 16:54	314, 346, 497
2:2	14:278–280	251
2:4	14:372, 388[c]; 15:94	286, 293[c], 341
2:7	15:312	442
2:9	15:252, 256, 310, 318	416, 417, 441, 445
2:10	14:204[c]; 15:6; 16:50–52	217[c], 300–301, 495
2:11	14:308; 15:20; 16:54	261, 307, 497
2:12	16:54	497
2:14	15:260, 276	419, 426
2:15	15:204; 16:154	394, 537
2:16	15:260	419
2:17	15:276	426
2:18	15:276, 304	426, 439
3:1	14:324; 15:288	268, 432
3:2	14:308, 324 (twice)	261, 268 (twice)
3:3	14:324	268
3:4	14:324 (twice); 15:6	268 (twice), 301
3:5	14:324	268
3:6	14:324; 16:62, 86, 228	268, 500, 509, 566
3:7	14:150[c], 366–368; 15:244, 356, 360	193[c], 285, 412, 457, 458
3:8	14:150[c]; 15:360	193[c], 458
3:13	16:320; 17:328	607, 772
3:14	16:4, 86	477, 509–510
4:2	15:364	460

4:9	17:174[c], 182	707[c], 711
4:10	17:174[c], 182	707[c], 711
4:11	17:182–184	711
4:12	15:40–42	318–319
4:13	14:56	150
4:15	15:276, 304	426, 439
5:2	15:276	426
5:4	15:284[c]	431[c]
5:5	14:184; 15:284	207, 431
5:6	14:184; 15:284[c]	207, 431[c]
5:7	14:328	270
5:8	14:328	270
5:10	15:290–292	433
5:11	17:44–46	654
5:13	16:16–18	482
5:14	16:16–18; 17:38	482, 651
6:1	14:20	128
6:2	14:20; 16:214; 17:176	128, 561, 708
6:3	14:20	128
6:4	15:342, 354, 356; 16:84[c]; 17:164	453, 457 (twice), 509[c], 702
6:5	16:84[c]	509[c]
6:6	15:342; 16:84	453, 509
6:10	15:336; 17:378	451, 791
6:11	15:408	476
6:13	17:120	684
6:16	17:120	685
6:17	14:74; 16:68	161, 503
6:18	14:48; 16:68, 70–72	146, 503, 504
6:19	16:70–72	504
6:20	16:70[c]	504[c]
7:2	15:300	436
7:3	14:310	262–263
7:9	15:182–184	385
7:10	15:44, 182–184	320, 385
7:12	16:128	527
7:15[o]	16:128[q]	527[q]
7:16[o]	16:128–130[q]	527[q]
7:17	15:292	433
7:18	16:130	527
7:19	16:114 [7:18]	522 [7:18]
7:20	15:292; 16:114 [7:19]	433, 522 [7:19]
7:21	15:292; 16:114 [7:20]	433, 522 [7:20]
7:22	15:316, 330; 16:114	444, 449, 522
7:23	16:206[c]	558[c]
7:24	15:274; 16:206[c], 210[c]	425, 558[c], 559[c]

7:25	15:274, 294, 402, 406; 16:210[c]	425, 434, 474, 475–476, 559[c]
7:26	15:196, 272–274, 280	390, 425, 428
7:27	15:272[c], 294; 16:210[c]	425[c], 434, 559[c]
7:28	15:274	425
8:1	15:294, 314	434, 442
8:2	15:294	434
8:3	15:276–278	426
8:5	16:102	517
8:6	14:280; 16:114	251, 522
8:8	15:298; 16:112	436, 522
8:9	16:112	522
8:10	16:114[q], 116	522[q], 523
8:13	16:130	527–528
9:8	14:368; 16:98	285, 515
9:9[o]	16:98–100[c]	515[c]
9:10[o]	16:98–100[c]	515[c]
9:12	15:292	434
9:14	14:364; 15:292, 330, 376	284, 434, 449, 464
9:15	15:330; 16:112–114, 210[q]	449, 522, 559[q]
9:16	16:112–114	522
9:22	15:278	426
9:24	15:294, 332	434, 449
9:25	15:294; 16:210[c]	434, 559[c]
9:26	15:294; 16:210[c]	434, 559[c]
9:28	15:292, 294, 322	433, 434, 446
10:5	14:236; 15:260, 276, 280	231, 419, 426, 428
10:6	15:280[c]	428[c]
10:7	15:260[q], 316	419[q], 443
10:9	15:284, 316	431, 443
10:10	15:284, 292, 294, 376; 16:210[c]	431, 434 (twice), 464, 559[c]
10:12	15:294, 316; 16:210[c]	434, 444, 559[c]
10:14	15:294, 328; 16:22, 210[c]	434, 449, 483, 559[c]
10:15	14:368, 382	285, 290
10:16	15:298	436
10:19	15:334	450
10:20	15:334	450
10:22	15:394, 406; 16:72; 17:42	472, 476, 504, 653
10:23	15:406; 16:72	476, 504
10:24	16:320	607
10:25	16:232	568
10:26	16:122	525
10:27	15:204; 16:122[q]	394, 525[q]
10:29	15:316, 326; 17:164	444, 447, 702
10:34	16:318, 378	606, 632
10:35	17:162	701

10:36	16:318; 17:66	606, 663
10:39	15:404	475
11	15:404	475[1]
11:1	15:394; 16:30	472, 487
11:3	14:44 (twice)[2]; 15:4, 16–18	144 (twice)[3]; 300, 306
11:4	16:34	488
11:6	14:28, 116; 15:362, 400, 406; 17:6, 10	132, 180, 459, 474, 476, 639, 641
11:7	15:398; 16:46	473, 493
11:10	15:32; 16:350	312, 620
11:11	15:400	474
11:16	15:32	312
11:19	15:398	473
11:22	17:262	745
11:23	17:400	800
11:24	17:240[c]	735[c]
11:25	17:240[c]	735[c]
11:26	16:318; 17:10–12, 240	606, 641, 735
11:31[o]	15:396 [11:3]	472 [11:3]
11:32	17:248	738
11:33[o]	17:248[x]	738[x]
11:36	16:316; 17:162	605, 702
12:2	15:288, 310, 314, 394; 16:16 [12:7]; 17:12	432, 441, 442, 471, 481–482, 641
12:3	17:46	654
12:7	15:388	469
12:8	15:388	469
12:9	15:50	323–324
12:12	17:46	654
12:14	16:42; 17:282	491, 754
12:18	16:130	528
12:19[o]	16:130[q]	528[q]
12:22	15:34; 16:54, 62, 130[q]	315, 497, 500, 528[q]
12:23	14:190; 16:54, 62	211, 497, 500
12:24[o]	16:130[q]	528[q]
12:28	17:58, 220	660, 727
13:2	17:382	792
13:3	17:272	749
13:4	15:144–146, 154; 17:290	366, 370, 756
13:5	17:224, 228	729, 731
13:7	17:420	807
13:8	14:18; 16:110	127, 520
13:9	16:304; 17:112	601, 681
13:13	17:240	735
13:16	17:344	779

13:17	17:420	807
13:18	17:40, 420	652, 807
13:20	15:256, 288, 368; 16:16, 64	417, 432, 462, 481, 501
13:21	16:16 (twice)	481 (twice)

James

1:2	15:88	339
1:3	15:88	339
1:4	16:18	482
1:5	17:28	648
1:6	15:394; 17:82	472, 669
1:7	17:82[c]	669[c]
1:9	17:242	736
1:10	17:242	736
1:12	15:88	339
1:13	15:72, 86	332, 338
1:14	15:72, 192; 17:202	332, 388, 720
1:15	15:192; 17:202[c]	388, 720[c]
1:17	14:46; 15:54–56, 354, 368[c]	144, 327, 457, 462[c]
1:18	14:106, 188; 15:368 (twice)	176, 210, 462 (twice)
1:21	16:118	524
1:22	14:22; 17:4	129, 637
1:25	16:42, 114, 154, 156	491, 522–523, 537 (twice)
1:26	17:194	716
1:27	14:240; 17:194	232, 716
2:2	17:364	786
2:7[1]	17:156	699
2:8	16:144	533
2:10	15:182	384
2:12	16:154, 156, 358	537, 539, 623
2:13	17:268	748
2:15	17:256	742
2:16	17:256[c]	742[c]
2:17	16:38[c]	490[c]
2:19	15:110, 362	349, 459
2:20	16:38[c]	490[c]
2:22	17:6	639
2:23	16:28	486
2:24	16:36–38, 42[q]	489–490, 491[q]
2:26	16:38[c]	490[c]
3:1	17:238	734
3:2	16:14; 17:210	481, 723
3:8	17:320	769
3:9	14:242	233

3:13	17:28	648
3:16	17:268	747
3:17	17:28	648
4:1	15:72	332
4:3	17:84	670–671
4:4	16:18–20; 17:52	482, 657
4:6	17:64[c]	662[c]
4:7	16:20	483
4:9	15:382	467
4:12	16:334; 17:396[c]	612, 798[c]
4:17	15:200	391
5:4	17:336	775
5:7	17:66	663
5:8	17:66	663
5:12	17:124[c], 130[c]	686[c], 688[c]
5:13	17:118	683
5:14	16:216[c]; 17:146	562[c], 695
5:15	16:216[c]	562[c]
5:16	15:384	468
5:19	17:328	772
5:20	17:282, 328[c]	753, 772[c]

1 Peter

1:2	14:96, 122, 234; 15:374, 376	171, 183, 231, 464 (twice)
1:3	14:188–190, 240[c]; 15:334, 368, 376, 406	210, 232[c], 450, 462, 464, 476
1:4	15:334; 16:376	450, 631
1:5	16:82	508
1:7	15:88	338
1:8	15:398–400; 16:74	473, 505
1:9	15:404; 16:74	475, 505
1:10	14:18; 15:290; 16:114, 116	127, 433, 523 (twice)
1:11	14:18, 368; 15:290	127, 285, 433
1:12	14:264–266, 374; 15:98; 16:114[q], 118[c]	244–245, 287, 344, 523[q], 524[c]
1:13	15:406; 17:212	476, 724
1:17	14:126; 17:60	184, 660
1:18[1]	15:316	444
1:19	14:88; 15:256	166, 417
1:20	14:88; 15:252	166, 416
1:21	14:236, 338, 356; 15:402, 408	231, 273, 280, 474, 476
1:23	15:366; 16:202	461, 557
2:2	16:18, 306	482, 601
2:4	14:338	273

2:6	14:98	172
2:7	14:154[c], 162–164, 174, 294, 296[q]	195[c], 198–199, 202, 257 (twice)[q]
2:8	14:92, 154[c], 162–164, 174	169, 195[c], 198–199, 202
2:9	15:346; 16:208[c], 244; 17:58	454, 558[c], 572, 660
2:11[o]	17:212 [2:12]	724 [2:12]
2:12	17:12	641
2:13	17:388, 400, 402	795, 799, 800
2:14	14:88; 17:402[c]	167, 800[c]
2:16	16:156	537
2:17	17:272, 294	749, 758
2:18	17:370, 402[c]	788, 800[c]
2:19	17:66–68, 370	663, 788
2:20[o]	17:66–68[x]	663[x]
2:21[o]	17:66–68[x]	663[x]
2:23[o]	17:66–68[x]	663[x]
2:24	15:292 (twice), 330; 16:10	433, 434, 449, 480
3:1	17:352	782
3:3	17:222	728
3:6	15:120	355
3:7	17:350	782
3:8	17:322	769
3:9	16:54; 17:256, 288	496–497, 742, 755
3:14	17:162, 206	702, 721–722
3:15	14:296; 17:162	257, 701
3:17	15:66	330
3:18	14:368; 15:256, 280, 292, 294, 308	285, 417, 427, 433, 434, 440
3:19	14:18, 368; 15:242[2], 290	126, 285, 410[3], 433
3:20	16:190	552
3:21	15:332; 16:168–170, 170[q], 190, 200	449, 544, 545[q], 552, 556
3:22	15:36, 98	315, 344
4:1	15:292	434
4:2	17:202	720
4:3	17:144, 216	694, 725
4:4	17:216	725
4:5	15:242	410
4:6	14:364; 15:242; 16:4	284, 410, 477
4:7	17:212	724
4:8	17:212–214, 272	724, 749
4:9	17:382	792
4:10	16:246; 17:362	572–573, 785–786
4:11	14:240, 338; 16:246	232, 273, 572–573
4:12	15:88, 338	338–339, 452
4:13	15:334	450
4:14	16:318	606
4:15[4]	17:364	786

4:16	16:318	606
4:19	15:66, 246	330, 413
5:1	16:228, 286, 288[c]	566, 593–594, 594[c]
5:2	15:212; 16:300; 17:46	397, 598, 654
5:3	16:244[5], 300[c], 310; 17:396	572, 598[c], 603, 798
5:4	16:64, 376	501, 631
5:5	17:64 (twice)[6]	662 (twice)[7]
5:6	17:64[c]	662[c]
5:8	15:108; 17:216	348, 726
5:10	15:344, 346 (twice); 16:66, 68, 376	454 (three times), 502, 503, 631

2 Peter

1:1	14:268; 15:400	245, 474
1:3	15:344; 16:66	454, 502
1:4	14:38, 196; 15:370; 16:68	137, 213, 462–463, 503
1:5	16:82; 17:4, 26	508, 637, 647
1:7	17:272	749
1:8[o]	16:82[x]; 17:4[x]	508[x], 637[x]
1:9	16:72	504
1:10	16:70, 72, 82[x]	503, 504, 508[x]
1:11	16:72	504
1:12	16:236, 254	569, 577
1:13	15:250	414
1:14	15:250	414
1:15	15:250; 16:254	414, 577
1:16	14:338	273
1:17	14:338, 348	273, 277
1:19	16:270	586
1:20	16:258–260	579–580
1:21	14:368, 388; 16:258–260	285, 292, 579–580
2:1	15:326; 17:418	447, 806
2:3	14:94	170
2:4	15:96, 106	343, 348
2:5	16:102	516
2:7	17:152[c]	697[c]
2:8	17:152[c]	697[c]
2:9	17:212	724
2:10	17:156[1], 212[x]	699[2], 724[x]
2:11	15:34, 102; 17:158[3]	315, 346, 699[4]
2:14	17:222	728
2:18	16:82	508
2:19	16:158	540
2:20	15:364; 16:82–84[x]	460, 508[x]
2:22	16:96	513

3:[0,5]	16:344	618
3:1	16:254	577
3:2	16:254[c]	577[c]
3:3	16:344	618
3:4	16:344	618
3:5	15:6, 36	301, 316
3:7	16:368–370	628
3:9	14:96, 150[c]; 15:318, 322	171, 193[c], 445, 446
3:10	16:370	628
3:12	16:370	628
3:13	16:380	633
3:15	16:254	577
3:16	16:254[c], 262	577[c], 581
3:18	14:338; 16:18	273, 482

1 John

1:3	16:58	498
1:6	16:58	498
1:7	15:260, 328–330, 376; 16:58	419, 449, 464, 498
1:8	16:14, 92	481, 512
1:9	15:336, 400	451, 474
2:1	14:240; 15:284, 294, 332	232, 430–431, 434, 449
2:2	15:286, 292, 320	431, 433, 446
2:3	14:24; 16:14; 17:28	129, 481, 648
2:4	17:8[c]	639[c]
2:5	17:70	664
2:9	17:274	749
2:10	17:272	749
2:11	17:274[c]	749[c]
2:14	16:20, 254; 17:250	483, 577, 739
2:15	14:242; 16:20; 17:52	233, 483, 657
2:16	14:242; 15:72	233, 332
2:17	16:80; 17:70	507, 664
2:18	16:314	604
2:19	16:88–90, 96, 220, 314[q]	510–511, 513, 563, 604[q]
2:20	14:316; 16:8, 270	265, 479, 586
2:21	16:254	577
2:23	16:56	498
2:24	16:86	510
2:25	16:120	524
2:27	16:8, 270–272	479, 586
2:28	16:80	507
2:29	15:372; 16:44	463, 492
3:1	14:270[c]; 16:52	246[c], 496

3:2	14:270[c]; 16:52 (twice), 376	246[c], 496 (twice), 631
3:3	16:14, 90–92	481, 511
3:4[1]	15:178	382
3:5[o]	14:270[c]	246[c]
3:6	16:22	483
3:7	16:42; 17:24	491–492, 646
3:8	14:270[c]; 15:96, 180, 252; 16:98	246[c], 343, 383, 415, 515
3:9	14:188; 15:372–374; 16:90, 94 (twice)[q]	210, 463, 511, 512–513[q], 513[q]
3:10	16:92; 17:196, 198	511, 717, 718
3:13	16:20	482
3:14	16:72, 94; 17:272	504, 513, 749
3:15	15:200; 17:258, 272[c], 286	391, 743, 749[c], 755
3:16	14:268[2]; 15:308; 17:270[c]	246[3], 440, 748[c]
3:18	17:196	717
3:19	17:40, 196	652, 717
3:21	17:40	652
3:23	14:22, 334; 15:402	129, 272, 474
3:24	16:56–58; 17:8[c]	498, 639[c]
4:2	15:260	419
4:3	16:314	604
4:7	17:196, 272	717, 749
4:8	14:58; 17:258, 272[c]	150–151, 743, 749[c]
4:9	14:104, 188, 224; 15:252, 286	175, 210, 227, 416, 431
4:10	14:104[c]; 15:252–254, 292	175[c], 416, 434
4:11	17:254	741
4:13	16:58, 118[c]	498, 524[c]
4:14	15:318	445
4:15	14:356; 16:58	280, 498
4:16	16:10, 58, 92	479, 498–499, 511
4:17	16:52	496
4:18	16:72; 17:62	504, 661
4:19	17:58	660
4:20	17:194	716
5:1	14:188, 356	210, 280
5:2	17:272	749
5:3	16:154; 17:70	537, 664
5:4	15:298, 300; 16:20, 154[c]	436, 437, 483, 537[c]
5:5	14:356, 400; 16:154[c]	280, 297, 537[c]
5:6[o]	14:400	297
5:7	14:214, 374, 398, 400[4]	221, 287, 297 (twice)
5:8[o]	14:398[5]	297
5:9	14:348	277
5:10	14:334	271–272
5:13	15:404	475

5:14	15:400	474
5:16	16:332; 17:98	611, 675
5:18	15:374; 16:22, 92	463–464, 483, 511–512
5:20	14:40, 270	140, 247
5:21	17:136[c], 144	691[c], 694

2 John

v. 1	14:98	172
v. 4	14:240[1]	232
v. 5	14:240[c]	232[c]
v. 6	14:240	232
v. 7	14:272[c]; 16:314	248[c], 604
v. 10	16:330	610
v. 11	16:330	610–611
v. 12	16:270	586
v. 13	14:98	172

3 John

v. 5	17:382	792
v. 6	17:382	792
v. 9	17:420	807
v. 10	16:330; 17:382	610, 793
v. 13	16:270[c]	586[c]

Jude

v. 1	16:76	505
v. 4	14:94, 274	170, 249
v. 6	15:96, 106, 180	343, 348, 383
v. 9	15:36, 104[1]	315, 347[2]
v. 14	16:338, 346	614, 618
v. 15	16:338	614
v. 16	17:230	731
v. 20	16:230; 17:84	567, 670
v. 22	16:328	610
v. 23	16:328[c]	610[c]
v. 24	16:68	503
v. 25	14:234; 15:254	230, 417

Revelation

1:1	14:290, 316	255, 265
1:3	16:258	578

1:4	14:38[1], 44, 394, 396; 15:102; 16:308	138, 143, 295, 296, 346, 602
1:5	14:182, 396; 15:256, 288, 296	207[2], 296, 417, 432, 435
1:6	14:240; 16:208[c], 244	232, 558[c], 572
1:7	14:298	258
1:8	14:48[3], 290, 318	145[4], 255, 266
1:10	17:186[c]	711[c]
1:11	14:290, 346	255, 276
1:13	14:292	255
1:17	14:292, 346; 15:308	255, 276–277, 440
1:18	15:308	440
1:19	16:254	577
1:20	16:200[c]	555[c]
2:1	16:228	566
2:2	16:306, 332	601, 611
2:7	14:292; 15:114; 16:20, 306	255[5], 353, 482–483, 601
2:8	14:346; 15:308	276–277, 440
2:9	15:392	470
2:10	15:88; 16:86	339, 510
2:11	16:20	483
2:14	16:316[c], 330; 17:142	605[c], 611, 693–694
2:17	16:72	504
2:20	17:142	694
2:23	14:316	265
2:25	16:360[c]	624[c]
2:26	14:318; 16:20, 42, 360	266, 483, 491, 624
2:27	14:318; 16:360	266, 624
3:1	14:122; 15:204	182, 394
3:3	17:216	726
3:4	15:336	451
3:5	14:116; 16:20	180, 483
3:7	16:328	609
3:8	16:328	609
3:11	16:86	510
3:12	14:346; 16:20	276–277, 483
3:14	14:182, 190, 192; 15:8	206, 211[6], 302
3:15	17:152[c]	697[c]
3:16	17:152[c]	697[c]
3:17	17:64	662
3:18	17:18	643
3:20	16:58	499
3:21	16:20	483
4	14:60	152
4:5	14:398; 15:102	296–297, 346
4:8	15:100	345

4:11	15:14	305
5:3	15:106	348
5:6	14:398; 15:102	296–297, 346
5:7	15:288	432
5:8	17:82	669
5:9	15:256, 322	417, 447
5:10	16:362, 380	625, 633
5:11	15:34, 98	315, 344
5:12	14:264, 332; 15:34, 98	243, 271, 315, 344
5:13	14:264	243–244
6:9	15:242	411
6:10	14:58; 17:288	151, 756
6:12	16:346–348	619
6:15[o,7]	16:348	619
6:16	16:348[8]; 17:42	619[9], 653
7:11	15:100	345
7:12	15:100	345
7:14	16:376	631
7:15	16:376–378	631
7:16	16:376–378	631
7:17	16:376[c]	631[c]
8:3	17:82	669
8:4	17:82	669
9:1	16:372	629
9:11	15:110	350
9:20	17:136	691
10:1	15:104	347
10:5	17:120	684
10:6	16:366, 370; 17:120	627, 628, 684
11:15	16:362	625
12:3	15:110	350
12:6	16:316	605
12:7	15:36 (twice), 104	315 (twice), 347
12:8	15:104 (twice)	347 (twice)
12:9	15:110 (twice)	349, 350
12:10[10]	15:110	350
12:11	16:20; 17:200	483, 719
12:12	15:108	348
12:14	16:316	605
13	16:314	604
13:3	14:142[c]	190[c]
13:5[11]	17:156	699
13:6	17:156[c]	699[c]
13:8	14:142; 15:256, 294	190, 417, 434
13:13	16:224	565

14:4	17:218	726
14:11	16:372	629
14:13	16:20	483
16:11[12]	17:156	699
16:15	17:216	726
17:9	16:200	555
17:12	16:200	555
17:14	15:300	437
19:2	16:314	604
19:3	16:372[c]	629[c]
19:7	16:64	500
19:8	16:28	486
19:9	15:350	456
19:10	17:144	694 [19:9]
19:13	14:254	239
19:16[o]	15:296	435
20:1[o]	16:362[c]	625[c]
20:2	15:110; 16:362[c]	349, 625[c]
20:3	15:108, 110; 16:362[c]	349 (twice), 625[c]
20:4[o]	16:362	625
20:5[o]	16:362	625
20:6[o]	16:362	625
20:7[13]	16:362 (twice)	625 (twice)
20:8	15:110; 16:362–364	349, 625
20:9	16:362–364	625
20:10	15:106	348
20:11	16:364	625–626
20:12	14:94; 16:354, 358, 364	170, 622, 623, 626
20:13	16:354, 364	622, 626
20:14[14]	16:364 (twice)	626 (twice)
20:15	16:364[c], 364–366, 372	626 (twice)[15], 629
21:1	16:370, 380	628, 633
21:2[o]	16:380[q]	633[q]
21:4	16:378	631
21:7	16:20	483
21:8	16:372 (twice); 17:250	629 (twice), 739
21:14	16:228[c]	567[c]
22:1	16:378	631
22:2[o]	16:378[c]	631[c]
22:3[o]	16:378[c]	631[c]
22:4[o]	16:378[c]	631[c]
22:5	16:378[c]	631[c]
22:6	14:292	255
22:8	14:292; 17:144[c]	255, 694[c]
22:9	14:292; 17:144[c]	255, 694[c]

22:12	14:292	255
22:13	14:292	255
22:14	14:292; 16:372	255–256, 629
22:15	16:372; 17:296	629, 759
22:16	14:292	256
22:18	16:280; 17:72	591, 665
22:19	14:116; 16:280–282; 17:72[c]	180, 591, 665[c]
22:20	14:332	271

Notes
Tables

Notes

Genesis

1 Milton quotes the Hebrew text of this verse.
2 Milton alludes to this verse but does not cite it or quote it.
3 Milton alludes to this verse but does not cite it or quote it.
4 Columbia cites the verse only not book and chapter.
5 Columbia cites the verse only not book and chapter.
6 Milton refers to the Hebrew text of this verse.
7 Milton refers to the Hebrew text of this verse.
8 Both Columbia and Yale, following a superscript correction in the manuscript of *De doctrina christiana*, cite this as Gen. 12:10.
9 Both Columbia and Yale, following a superscript correction in the manuscript of *De doctrina christiana*, cite this as Gen. 12:10.
10 Milton refers here to the Hebrew text of this verse.
11 Milton alludes to events in this chapter, but he does not specifically cite it or quote from it.
12 This allusion does not specifically cite the location.
13 This allusion does not specifically cite the location.

Exodus

1 Milton alludes to the events in this chapter but does not cite it.
2 Milton alludes to the events in this chapter but does not cite it.
3 Milton quotes the Hebrew text of this verse.
4 Milton quotes the Hebrew text of this verse.
5 The first time this verse occurs on this page Milton cites it but does not quote it.
6 The first time this verse occurs on this page Milton cites it but does not quote it.
7 The first time this verse occurs on this page Milton cites it but does not quote it.
8 The first time this verse occurs on this page Milton cites it but does not quote it.
9 Milton refers to the Hebrew text of this verse.
10 Milton refers to the Hebrew text of this verse.
11 Milton refers to the Hebrew text of this verse.

Leviticus

1 This allusion does not specifically cite the location.
2 This allusion does not specifically cite the location.
3 The first time this verse occurs on this page it is cited but not quoted.

Numbers

1 Although I cannot be sure (because Milton cites this verse but does not quote it), I believe he is referring to Num. 23:5, 16. I have followed both Columbia and Yale, however, where it is cited as Num. 23:8, 20.
2 Although I cannot be sure (because Milton cites this verse but does not quote it), I believe he is referring to Num. 23:5, 16. I have followed both Columbia and Yale, however, where it is cited as Num. 23:8, 20.
3 Although I cannot be sure (because Milton cites this verse but does not quote it), I believe he is referring to Num. 23:5, 16. I have followed both Columbia and Yale, however, where it is cited as Num. 23:8, 20.

Deuteronomy

1 Both times this verse occurs on this page it is cited but not quoted.
2 The second allusion is made without specific citation of the location.
3 The second allusion is made without specific citation of the location.
4 Though Milton quotes Deut. 18:15, 16, only verse 15 is cited.
5 Though Milton quotes Deut. 18:15, 16, only verse 15 is cited.
6 Although Milton cites Deut. 27:13 to the end of the chapter, he quotes only from verse 13.
7 The first time this verse occurs on this page, it is cited but not quoted.
8 The first time this verse occurs on this page, it is cited but not quoted.
9 Columbia omits this reference.

Joshua

1 Milton alludes to events in this chapter, but he does not cite it or quote from it.

Judges

1 Milton quotes the Hebrew text of this verse.
2 Milton quotes the Hebrew text of this verse.

1 Samuel

1 Milton alludes to this verse but does not quote it or cite its exact location.
2 Milton alludes to this verse but does not quote it or cite its exact location.

2 Samuel

1 Milton alludes to this verse but does not quote it or cite its exact location.
2 Milton alludes to this verse but does not quote it or cite its exact location.

3 The second allusion is made without specific reference to the location.
4 This allusion contains no specific reference to the location.
5 Milton alludes to this chapter but does not cite its location.

1 Kings

1 Milton alludes to this verse but does not cite its location.
2 Milton alludes to this verse but does not cite its location.
3 Milton alludes to the events of this chapter but does not cite it.
4 Milton alludes to this verse but does not cite it or quote it.
5 Milton alludes to this verse but does not cite it or quote it.
6 Milton alludes to this verse but does not cite it or quote it.
7 Milton alludes to this verse but does not cite it or quote it.
8 Milton alludes to this verse but does not cite it or quote it.

2 Kings

1 Milton alludes to the events of this chapter but does not cite it.
2 Milton alludes to this chapter but does not cite it.

1 Chronicles

1 Milton alludes to, but does not quote, this chapter.

2 Chronicles

1 The second time this verse occurs on this page, it is cited but not quoted.

Nehemiah

1 Yale, following the manuscript, cites this as Neh. 8:9.
2 Yale, following the manuscript, cites this as Neh. 8:10.

Job

1 Although Milton cites Job 3:12–18, he quotes only verse 16.
2 This verse is cited in Columbia but not quoted. Yale does not cite this verse at this point.
3 This verse is cited in Columbia but not quoted. Yale does not cite this verse at this point.
4 Though Milton quotes Job 29:11, 12, he cites Job 29:11 to the end of the chapter (i.e. verse 25).
5 Though Milton quotes Job 29:11, 12, he cites Job 29:11 to the end of the chapter (i.e. verse 25).
6 Though Milton quotes Job 29:11, 12, he cites Job 29:11 to the end of the chapter (i.e. verse 25).

Psalms

1 This allusion is made by the biblical writer whom Milton quotes (Acts 13:33).
2 This allusion is made by the biblical writer whom Milton quotes (Acts 13:33).

3 While Milton quotes only Psalm 5:4, both Columbia and Yale cite this as Psalm 5:5, 6, 7.
4 While Milton quotes only Psalm 5:4, both Columbia and Yale cite this as Psalm 5:5, 6, 7.
5 Milton quotes the Hebrew text of this verse.
6 Milton cites, but does not quote, Psalm 12:3, which is listed here as Psalm 12:2.
7 Milton quotes the Hebrew text of this verse.
8 Milton quotes this verse but does not cite its exact location. (According to his usual designation, it would be cited as Psalm 18:43. His actual citation reads Psalm 18:38–43.)
9 Milton quotes this verse but does not cite its exact location. (According to his usual designation, it would be cited as Psalm 18:43. His actual citation reads Psalm 18:38–43.)
10 Milton does not identify this allusion. My identification is conjectural. He could be alluding instead to Jer. 37:20.
11 Both Columbia and Yale cite these verses as "Psalm 34:19, etc."
12 Both Columbia and Yale cite these verses as "Psalm 34:19, etc."
13 Both Columbia and Yale cite this as Psalm 40:7. Confusion may arise from the fact that the writer of Hebrews, whom Milton quotes, is himself quoting from the LXX version of Psalm 40:6, 7, where the wording is quite different.
14 Yale omits this reference at this point.
15 Milton quotes John 10:34, which itself quotes this verse. Milton makes reference to this quotation by Jesus as originating from the book of Psalms.
16 Milton quotes John 10:34, which itself quotes this verse. Milton makes reference to this quotation by Jesus as originating from the book of Psalms.
17 Milton quotes the Hebrew text of this verse.
18 Milton alludes to, but does not quote, Psalm 88:10–12. Both Columbia and Yale cite these verses as Psalm 88:11–13.
19 Milton alludes to, but does not quote, Psalm 88:10–12. Both Columbia and Yale cite these verses as Psalm 88:11–13.
20 Milton alludes to, but does not quote, Psalm 88:10–12. Both Columbia and Yale cite these verses as Psalm 88:11–13.
21 Both Columbia and Yale cite this as Psalm 102:28 the first time it occurs on this page. The second reference, however, is noted as Psalm 102:27.
22 Both Columbia and Yale cite this as Psalm 102:28 the first time it occurs on this page. The second reference, however, is noted as Psalm 102:27.
23 Milton quotes the Hebrew text of this verse.
24 Milton quotes the Hebrew text of this verse.
25 Milton quotes the Hebrew text of this verse.
26 Milton quotes the Hebrew text of this verse.

Proverbs

1 The first time this verse occurs on this page, Milton cites it but does not quote it.
2 Yale cites the book and chapter only, not the verse.
3 Although Milton cites Prov. 31:1–10, he quotes only from verse 1.

Isaiah

1 Yale does not cite this verse.

2 Both Columbia and Yale have misread the manuscript at this point and cited this and the following verse as Isa. 31:2 rather than Isa. 3:1, 2.
3 The second reference to this verse is cited in Yale as Isa. 6:22.
4 Milton cites this verse as Isa. 27:15, but he does not quote it.
5 Though Milton cites Isa. 53:4–11, he quotes only from verse 11.
6 Though Milton cites Isa. 53:4–11, he quotes only from verse 11.

Jeremiah

1 Milton refers to Jer. 32:37–44, but he only cites verse 37 by number.

Ezekiel

1 Although Milton cites Ezekiel 13, he quotes only from verse 2.
2 Milton's reference here is to the Vulgate text.
3 Although Milton cites chapter 33 from verse 2 to the end of the chapter ("et 33 toto cap. a v. 2"), he quotes only from verse 2.

Daniel

1 Milton alludes to the events in this chapter but does not cite it.

Amos

1 Milton cites the first eight verses of this chapter but does not quote from any of them. I, therefore, have entered this as a citation of the chapter.

Haggai

1 Both Columbia and Yale cite this as Hag. 2:7, although the quotation comes from verse 6 as well.

Malachi

1 Yale cites the chapter only.
2 Yale cites the chapter only.
3 Although Milton cites Mal. 2:1–10, he quotes only from verse 1.

Matthew

1 Milton refers here to the Greek text of this verse.
2 Milton refers here to the Greek text of this verse.
3 Milton refers here to the Greek text of this verse.
4 Milton refers here to the Greek text of this verse.
5 Milton's reference here is to the Greek text.
6 Milton's reference here is to the Greek text.
7 Milton's quotation here is from the Greek text.
8 Milton's quotation here is from the Greek text.
9 At 14:396, Columbia cites the verse location for Matt. 12:24–32 only, not the book and chapter.

10 Columbia does not refer to the chapter, only the verse.
11 Yale quotes this verse and the previous one, but cites only that verse.
12 The first time this verse occurs on this page, it is quoted but not cited.
13 Milton refers here to the beheading of John the Baptist, but he neither cites nor quotes the exact verses he has in mind. The accounts of John's death are found in Matt. 14:1–14, Mark 6:14–29, and Luke 9:7–9. I have entered the reference here as an allusion to Matt. 14 in general.
14 Milton's reference here is to the Greek text.
15 Milton's reference here is to the Greek text.
16 The first time this verse occurs on this page it is cited but not quoted.
17 The first time this verse occurs on this page it is cited but not quoted.
18 Columbia cites the verse only, not book or chapter.
19 Milton's second quotation of this verse on this page occurs without specific reference to its location.
20 Columbia cites the verse only, not book or chapter.
21 Columbia cites the verse only, not book or chapter.
22 Columbia cites the verse only, not book or chapter.
23 Columbia cites the verse only, not book or chapter.
24 Milton quotes the Greek text of this verse.
25 Milton quotes the Greek text of this verse.
26 Milton cites Matt. 24:3–27 twice on this page, but does not quote from it either time. I have cited it here as a reference to the chapter and not to the individual verses.
27 The second time this verse occurs on this page, Milton cites it but does not quote it.
28 Milton alludes here to Christ's parable of the foolish virgins (Matt. 25:1–13), which I have listed here as an allusion to the chapter.
29 Columbia cites this by verse only, not by book or chapter.
30 Columbia cites this by verse only, not by book or chapter.
31 The second allusion is to the Greek and Syriac versions of this verse.
32 The second allusion is to the Greek and Syriac versions of this verse.
33 Columbia cites only the verse location, not the book and chapter.

Mark

1 The second time this verse occurs on this page, Milton cites it but does not quote it.
2 Columbia cites the chapter only.
3 Milton alludes to this verse but does not quote it or cite it.
4 Milton alludes to this verse but does not quote it or cite it.
5 Milton alludes to this verse but does not quote it or cite it.
6 Milton alludes to this verse but does not quote it or cite it.
7 Milton alludes to this verse but does not quote it or cite it.
8 Milton alludes to this verse but does not quote it or cite it.
9 Milton alludes to this verse but does not quote it or cite it.
10 Milton alludes to this verse but does not quote it or cite it.
11 On the first occurrence of this verse on this page, Milton quotes it but does not cite it.

12 On the first occurrence of this verse on this page, Milton quotes it but does not cite it.

Luke

1 Milton quotes here from the Greek text of this verse.
2 Milton quotes here from the Greek text of this verse.
3 Milton alludes to this verse but does not quote it or cite it.
4 Milton's reference here is to the Greek text of this verse. (This is not obvious in the Yale edition.)
5 Both Columbia and Yale (following the manuscript) cite this as Luke 9:66.
6 Milton's reference here is to the Greek text of this verse. (This is not obvious in the Yale edition.)
7 Both Columbia and Yale (following the manuscript) cite this as Luke 9:66.
8 Columbia does not cite the exact book, chapter, and verse at this place.

John

1 Milton quotes the Greek text of this verse.
2 Milton quotes the Greek text of this verse.
3 Milton alludes here to the feeding of the five thousand, which is found in John 6:1–14. Because he has not specified the exact verses to which he is alluding, I have designated it here as a reference to the chapter.
4 Milton alludes here to the feeding of the five thousand, which is found in John 6:1–14. Because he has not specified the exact verses to which he is alluding, I have designated it here as a reference to the chapter.
5 Milton quotes the Greek text of this verse.
6 Milton quotes the Greek text of this verse.
7 The second time this verse occurs on this page Milton cites it but does not quote it.
8 The first time this verse occurs on this page Milton cites it but does not quote it.
9 Milton alludes to the story of the woman taken in adultery, which runs from the last verse of chapter 7 through the eleventh verse of chapter 8. Because he does not cite its specific location, I have cited it here as an allusion to chapter 8.
10 Milton quotes the Greek text of this verse.
11 Milton quotes the Greek text of this verse.
12 Milton alludes to this verse but does not quote it or cite it.
13 Milton alludes to this verse but does not quote it or cite it.
14 Yale does not include this citation.
15 Milton alludes to this verse but does not quote it or cite its location.
16 Milton alludes to this verse but does not quote it or cite its location.

Acts

1 Milton quotes the Greek text of this verse.
2 Milton quotes the Greek text of this verse.
3 Columbia cites Milton's quotation of Acts 5:30–31 as Acts 5:30, 31, 32, 33, though Milton cites only the first two verses.

4 Yale cites Milton's quotation of Acts 5:30–31 as Acts 5:30–35.
5 Yale cites this verse as Acts 10:34 the first time it occurs on this page.
6 In the first instance, Columbia refers only to the book, not the chapter. In the second, no specific location is mentioned.
7 The second time this verse appears on this page it is cited but not quoted.
8 The second time this verse appears on this page it is cited but not quoted.
9 Both Columbia and Yale cite this as Acts 13:46. (Columbia cites the verse only, not the book or the chapter.)
10 Milton quotes the Greek text of this verse.
11 Milton quotes the Greek text of this verse.
12 Milton refers here to the Vulgate text.
13 Milton refers here to the Vulgate text.
14 The first occurrence of this verse on this page is cited but not quoted.
15 Milton refers to both the Syriac and the Greek texts of this verse.
16 Milton refers to both the Syriac and the Greek texts of this verse.

Romans

1 Milton quotes the Greek text of this verse.
2 Milton quotes the Greek text of this verse.
3 Milton quotes the Greek text of this verse.
4 Although Milton quotes from Rom. 3:22–25, he cites only verse 22 specifically.
5 Although Milton quotes from Rom. 3:22–25, he cites only verse 22 specifically.
6 Although Milton quotes from Rom. 3:22–25, he cites only verse 22 specifically.
7 Although Milton quotes from Rom. 3:22–25, he cites only verse 22 specifically.
8 Although Milton quotes from Rom. 3:22–25, he cites only verse 22 specifically.
9 Although Milton quotes from Rom. 3:22–25, he cites only verse 22 specifically.
10 In the first of these references, Milton cites this verse but does not quote it.
11 In the first of these references, Milton cites this verse but does not quote it.
12 Milton's reference is to the Greek text of this verse.
13 Milton's reference is to the Greek text of this verse.
14 Milton alludes to this verse but does not quote it or cite its specific location.
15 Milton alludes to this verse but does not quote it or cite its specific location.
16 Only the first occurrence of this verse on this page is cited but not quoted.
17 Only the first occurrence of this verse on this page is cited but not quoted.
18 Yale cites the specific chapter; Columbia does not.
19 Columbia cites the verse only, not the book or the chapter.
20 Yale does not cite the book, only the chapter and verse.
21 Columbia cites the verse only, not the book or the chapter.
22 Yale does not cite the book, only the chapter and verse.
23 Columbia cites the verse only, not the book or the chapter.
24 Columbia cites the verse only, not the book or the chapter.
25 Columbia cites the verse only, not the book or the chapter.
26 Columbia cites the verse only, not the book or chapter.
27 Columbia cites the verse only, not the book or chapter.
28 Columbia does not cite the specific location of this verse.
29 Milton cites "from verse 4 to the end of the chapter" (i.e. Rom. 12:4–21) but does not quote from that passage. Therefore, I have listed it here not as a reference to any particular verse, but as a reference to the chapter.

30 The second time this verse occurs on this page it is quoted but its exact location is not given.
31 Milton cites Rom. 15:1–15. I have included it here as a citation to the chapter only, not to the individual verses themselves.

1 Corinthians

1 Milton quotes this verse but cites it as 1 Cor. 1:18 (i.e. after quoting 1 Cor. 1:17, he quotes this verse but refers to it as "sequens versus"– *De doctrina christiana* manuscript p. 359).
2 The second time this verse occurs on this page, it is cited but not quoted.
3 The second time this verse occurs on this page, it is cited but not quoted.
4 Although Milton cites verses 7–13, he quotes only from verse 7.
5 Although Milton cites verses 7–13, he quotes only from verse 7.
6 The second time this verse occurs on this page it is cited but not quoted.
7 The second time this verse occurs on this page it is cited but not quoted.
8 The second time this verse occurs on this page Milton cites it but does not quote it.
9 The second time this verse occurs on this page, it is cited but not quoted.
10 The second time this verse occurs on this page, it is cited but not quoted.
11 Milton quotes the Greek text of this verse.
12 Milton quotes the Greek text of this verse.

2 Corinthians

1 Milton alludes to this verse but does not quote it or cite it.
2 Milton alludes to this verse but does not quote it or cite it.
3 Milton alludes to this verse but does not quote it or cite it.
4 Milton alludes to this verse but does not quote it or cite it.
5 Both Columbia and Yale cite the book and chapter only, not the verse.
6 Both Columbia and Yale cite the book and chapter only, not the verse.
7 Milton quotes the Greek text of this verse.
8 Milton quotes the Greek text of this verse.
9 Though Columbia (English, 15:247) and Yale (413) quote Milton as citing 2 Cor. 5:1–20, he does not. They do so on the basis of Sumner's misreading of the manuscript and his subsequent conjectural interpolation and emendation. He adds "vigessimum" to his text (15:246) in order to make sense out of Milton's citation, which actually reads 2 Cor. 5:1–10, not 2 Cor. 5:1–20. Sumner has misread Skinner's handwriting here, mistaking his "1" for a "2," and rather than employing the numeral "20" (as he misread it), Sumner substitutes "vigessimum." The mistake, while understandable, is surprising. Sumner was able to read Skinner correctly in places where the orthography was far more ambiguous. On the very next manuscript page, for example, where Skinner has written "2 Pet. 1," the numerals are strikingly similar, yet Sumner reads them aright.
10 Both Columbia and Yale (following the *De doctrina christiana* manuscript) cite this as "2 Cor. 6:3, etc."
11 Milton quotes the Greek text of this verse.
12 The first time the verse occurs on this page it is cited but not quoted.

Galatians

1 Both Columbia and Yale fail to italicize this quotation.
2 Both Columbia and Yale fail to italicize this quotation.
3 Both Columbia and Yale fail to italicize this quotation.
4 Both Columbia and Yale fail to italicize this quotation.
5 Milton's reference here is to the Greek text.
6 Milton's reference here is to the Greek text.
7 Milton's reference here is to the Greek text.
8 Milton's reference here is to the Greek text.

Ephesians

1 The second time this verse occurs on this page it is cited but not quoted.
2 The second time this verse occurs on this page it is cited but not quoted.
3 Milton quotes from the Greek text of this verse.
4 Milton quotes from the Greek text of this verse.
5 Milton quotes from the Greek text of this verse.
6 Milton quotes from the Greek text of this verse.
7 Milton quotes this verse but does not cite its location by verse number.
8 Milton quotes this verse but does not cite its location by verse number.
9 The second time this verse occurs on this page Milton cites it but does not quote it.
10 Milton quotes this verse but does not cite its location by verse number.
11 Milton quotes this verse but does not cite its location by verse number.
12 Milton quotes this verse but does not cite its location by verse number.
13 The second time this verse occurs on this page it is cited but not quoted.
14 Milton quotes this verse but does not cite it. He could be quoting, however, from Eph. 6:13. The Greek word Milton quotes (πανοπλία) in the *De doctrina christiana* manuscript p. 267 is found in both verses 11 and 13 (πανοπλίαν).

Philippians

1 Yale misspells this as Phillip. 2:6.
2 Milton quotes the Greek text of this verse.
3 Milton quotes the Greek text of this verse.
4 Yale misspells this as Phillip. 2:13.
5 Yale misspells this as Phillip. 4:3.

Colossians

1 Milton quotes here from the Greek text of this verse.
2 Milton quotes here from the Greek text of this verse.
3 Milton quotes here from the Greek text of this verse.
4 Milton quotes here from the Greek text of this verse.
5 Milton quotes the Greek text of this verse.
6 Milton quotes the Greek text of this verse.

1 Timothy

1 Milton quotes the Greek text of this verse.
2 Milton quotes the Greek text of this verse.
3 Although Milton quotes only from verse 3, he cites verses 3–16.
4 Milton quotes the Greek text of this verse.
5 Milton quotes the Greek text of this verse.

2 Timothy

1 Milton quotes the Greek text of this verse.
2 Milton quotes the Greek text of this verse.
3 Milton quotes the Greek text of this verse.

Philemon

1 Milton refers here to the entire brief epistle.
2 Milton refers here to the entire brief epistle.
3 Columbia cites this as chapter 4 rather than verse 4 (i.e. Philemon iv.5).

Hebrews

1 Yale does not cite this chapter.
2 Milton's reference alludes also to the Syriac version of this verse.
3 Milton's reference alludes also to the Syriac version of this verse.

James

1 Milton's reference here is to the Vulgate text.

1 Peter

1 Milton quotes the Greek text of this verse.
2 Milton's reference here is to the original Greek version of this verse and to its translation in the Syriac version.
3 Milton's reference here is to the original Greek version of this verse and to its translation in the Syriac version.
4 Milton quotes the Greek text of this verse.
5 As does Milton in the *De doctrina christiana* manuscript, Columbia also cites verse 2, but does not quote it. Yale cites and quotes only verse 3.
6 The second time this verse occurs on this page, it is cited but not quoted.
7 The second time this verse occurs on this page, it is cited but not quoted.

2 Peter

1 Milton's reference here is to the Greek text.
2 Milton's reference here is to the Greek text.
3 Milton's reference here is to the Greek text.
4 Milton's reference here is to the Greek text.

5 Milton refers to 2 Pet. 3:3–18, but specifically cites and quotes only from verses 3 and 4. I have listed verses 3 and 4 separately and listed the remainder as a reference to the chapter.

1 John

1 Milton refers to the Greek text of this verse.
2 Milton refers to the Syriac text of this verse as well as to the Greek.
3 Milton refers to the Syriac text of this verse as well as to the Greek.
4 Columbia quotes this verse without citing its location.
5 Columbia quotes this verse without citing its location.

2 John

1 Columbia cites this as chapter 4, not verse 4 (i.e. 2 Ep. iv. 5, 6).

Jude

1 Milton's citation mentions the book only, not the verse.
2 Milton's citation mentions the book only, not the verse.

Revelation

1 Columbia cites only the chapter location, not the verse.
2 Yale, following the Columbia English, cites this as Rev. 1:4. The Latin text cites the chapter only.
3 Milton quotes the Greek text of this verse.
4 Milton quotes the Greek text of this verse.
5 Yale cites this as Rev. 2:17. The attribution is justifiable in that both Rev. 2:7 and 17 contain the words to which Milton alludes.
6 Though Columbia cites this verse twice at this location, Yale cites it once.
7 Milton quotes this verse as from Rev. 6, but he does not cite the specific verse number.
8 Milton quotes this verse as from Rev. 6, but he does not cite the specific verse number.
9 Milton quotes this verse as from Rev. 6, but he does not cite the specific verse number.
10 Milton quotes from the Greek text of this verse.
11 Milton refers here to the Vulgate text.
12 Milton refers here to the Vulgate text.
13 The first time this verse occurs on this page it is cited but not quoted.
14 The first time this verse occurs on this page it is cited but not quoted.
15 The first time this verse occurs on this page it is cited but not quoted.

Biblical citations in De doctrina christiana arranged by chapter

Table I

The following table computes the total number of Milton's biblical citations and distributes them according to their location in Milton's text and according to their respective canonical books. The columns designate, from left to right, the chapter in Milton's *De doctrina*, the number of verse citations in that chapter, the number of chapter citations, and the total number of citations. For example, a reference to Matt. 13:1–3 is counted as a reference to three verses.

The reader should bear in mind that because Milton's references sometimes are ambiguous, and because that ambiguity can be construed in different ways by prospective indexers, these numbers, while specific, must not be taken as unqualified absolutes. Their very specificity veils an occasional ambiguity. Given that proviso, however, these numbers are reliable indicators of Milton's citational practices.

Book One

DDC	VERSE CITATIONS	CHAPTER CITATIONS	TOTAL
Epistle	3	0	3
Ch. 1	50	0	50
Ch. 2	241	4	245
Ch. 3	52	0	52
Ch. 4	327	9	336
Pref., Ch. 5	0	0	0
Ch. 5	796	1	797
Ch. 6	220	2	222
Ch. 7	231[1]	6	237[1]
Ch. 8	237	4	241
Ch. 9	138	3	141
Ch. 10	181	7	188

Ch. 11	110	2	112
Ch. 12	76	0	76
Ch. 13	179	2	181
Ch. 14	159	0	159
Ch. 15	185	1	186
Ch. 16	262	5	267[2]
Ch. 17	170[3]	0	170[3]
Ch. 18	85	0	85
Ch. 19	102	2	104
Ch. 20	109	1	110
Ch. 21	138	1	139
Ch. 22	129	3	132
Ch. 23	36	0	36
Ch. 24	55	0	55
Ch. 25	153	0	153
Ch. 26	86	1	87
Ch. 27	299	2	301
Ch. 28	220	3	223
Ch. 29	167	0	167
Ch. 30	165[4]	2	167[4]
Ch. 31	226	1	227
Ch. 32	96	2	98
Ch. 33	330	5	335
	6,013	69	6,082

Book Two

DDC	VERSE CITATIONS	CHAPTER CITATIONS	TOTAL
Ch. 1	116	3	119
Ch. 2	188	0	188
Ch. 3	218	5	223
Ch. 4	357	3	360
Ch. 5	207	2	209
Ch. 6	103	0	103
Ch. 7	85	1	86
Ch. 8	148	1	149
Ch. 9	316	3	319
Ch. 10	65	0	65
Ch. 11	233	4	237
Ch. 12	126	0	126

Ch. 13	235	6	241
Ch. 14	134	1	135
Ch. 15	242	3[5]	245
Ch. 16	102	2	104
Ch. 17	342	17	359
	3,217	51	3,268

Total References, Books One and Two 9,350

Verses cited by Milton five or more times, arranged in order of frequency

Table II

FREQUENCY	VERSES
12	Matt. 28:19; John 3:16
9	Rom. 3:25, 8:29; 1 Cor. 8:6
8	John 8:44; Rom. 2:15, 8:30
7	Mal. 3:1; Matt. 11:27; John 1:18, 16:13, 17:3; Acts 20:28; Rom. 5:10, 8:15; 2 Cor. 5:19; Eph. 1:11; Col. 1:16, 1:18; 2 Thes. 1:7; Tit. 3:5; Heb. 1:3, 11:6; 1 Pet. 5:10
6	Gen. 3:15, 17:1; Ex. 21:10; Psalm 2:7; Isa. 42:1; Jer. 31:33; Matt. 10:28, 20:28, 25:41, 28:20; John 1:12, 20:22; Acts 5:31, 14:17; Rom. 1:19, 8:16, 10:14, 12:2; 1 Cor. 1:9, 2:7, 6:11; 2 Cor. 5:10, 5:21; Gal. 3:13, 4:4; Eph. 1:4, 1:5, 1:10, 4:24, 5:26; Phil. 2:6; Col. 1:15, 2:2, 3:10; Heb. 1:2, 12:2; 1 Pet. 1:3, 3:18; Rev. 1:4.
5	Gen. 2:17, 3:16; Deut. 6:4; Neh. 9:6; Psalm 110:1; Jer. 31:31; Matt. 12:28, 15:19, 16:17, 18:19, 24:36, 28:18; Mark 13:32, 16:16; Luke 7:30; John 1:1, 1:9, 1:17, 3:5,

3:6, 5:22, 14:23, 17:5; Acts 2:42; Rom. 1:20, 2:14, 3:27, 3:28, 4:12, 8:3, 8:28, 8:34, 11:36; 1 Cor. 8:4, 12:13; 2 Cor. 3:3, 4:6; Gal. 4:6, 5:22; Eph. 2:5, 2:20, 3:10, 3:17; Phil. 2:7, 2:8, 2:9; Col. 2:14, 3:9; 1 Thes. 4:16; 2 Thes. 2:13; 1 Tim. 1:19, 6:14, 6:16; 2 Tim. 1:9, 2:13, 4:8; Tit. 1:2, 2:14; Heb. 1:5, 1:6, 3:7, 6:4, 7:25, 10:10, 13:20; 1 Pet. 1:2, 1:12, 1:21, 2:7, 3:21; 1 John 3:8, 3:9, 4:9; Rev. 1:5

A comparison between citations in Milton's De doctrina and John Calvin's Institutes arranged in canonical order

Table III

The following comparative chart is based upon the Yale edition of Milton's *De doctrina christiana* and upon the citations listed in Leroy Nixon, *Complete Indexes to the Institutes of the Christian Religion by John Calvin*, Grand Rapids: Wm. B. Eerdmans Pub. Co., 1950.

Old Testament

TEXT	MILTON	CALVIN
Genesis	311	233[1]
Exodus	245	112
Leviticus	94	20[1]
Numbers	79	25
Deuteronomy	264	116[1]
Joshua	41	20
Judges	43	31
Ruth	6	1
1 Samuel	94	45
2 Samuel	57	32
1 Kings	94	52

2 Kings	66	46
1 Chronicles	35	1
2 Chronicles	98	5
Ezra	13	0
Nehemiah	42	3
Esther	17	0
Job	167	54
Psalms	541	486
Proverbs	473	71
Ecclesiastes	85	13
Song of Solomon	5	1
Isaiah	320	288
Jeremiah	218	127
Lamentations	14	4
Ezekiel	128	87
Daniel	77	34
Hosea	31	21
Joel	9	18
Amos	32	14
Obadiah	1	1
Jonah	12	6
Micah	26	5
Nahum	1	0
Habakkuk	12	9
Zephaniah	7	4
Haggai	5	10
Zechariah	44	12
Malachi	28	32
	3,835	2,039

Apocrypha

Tobit	0	2
Wisdom of Solomon	1	1
Ecclesiasticus	0	2
Baruch	0	3
1 Maccabees	1	2
2 Maccabees	5	2
	7	12

New Testament

Matthew	631	392
Mark	114	34
Luke	299	178
John	641	329
Acts	434	300
Romans	582	480
1 Corinthians	412	366
2 Corinthians	222	153
Galatians	154	152[1]
Ephesians	263	245
Philippians	104	81
Colossians	141	116
1 Thessalonians	75	27
2 Thessalonians	76	36
1 Timothy	148	100
2 Timothy	62	36
Titus	63	46
Philemon	6	0
Hebrews	342	227
James	85	36
1 Peter	165	81
2 Peter	73	16
1 John	158	70
2 John	10	0
3 John	6	0
Jude	19	5
Revelation	219	17
	5,504	3,523
Grand Total	9,346[2]	5,574

Notes to Table I

1 This number includes two citations from Apocryphal texts.
2 This number does not include two general book citations, one to Matthew and one to Mark (Yale p. 442).
3 This number includes an allusion to four Apocryphal verses.
4 This number includes one citation from an Apocryphal text, which both Columbia and Yale cite as two verses.
5 This number includes an allusion to the book of Philemon, which is only one chapter long.

Notes to Table III

1 This number includes a large multiple verse reference which I have counted as a single reference to the chapter.
2 The reason for the four-verse discrepancy between this total and that recorded for Table I is that Table III is completed solely on the basis of the Yale edition.